MW01286754

The Empowered Cancer Journey

Knowing, Doing, Surviving
The Intuitive Approach to Healing

By Carol Lynne Fouad, Survivor

Copyright © 2019 Carol Fouad
ISBN-13: 9781073418473
All rights reserved.

Table of Contents

Foreword

We are all human; as a result, we all experience feeling and thoughts, and we inevitably act upon them for better or for worse. We are also prone to developing chronic illness, including, at an ever-increasing rate, cancer. It is estimated that, in our lifetime, one in three women will come down with this disease, and for men, it will be even more likely: one in two. As a functional integrative family medicine physician helping support patients with chronic illness, including cancer, I have come to appreciate how important emotions, thoughts, and actions are to one's overall well-being. That is why this book is so important and timely.

Carol Fouad, cancer survivor, lays out a clear and spirited recipe for success in helping to overcome a cancer diagnosis. The pages of this book are so raw and insightful that they can only be written by a cancer survivor. With Carol's thoughtful and intuitive sense, this book shares with the reader a deeply inspiring, at times painful, but ultimately successful story of knowing, doing, and surviving a cancer diagnosis.

Understanding how vulnerable one can be soon after such a diagnosis, Carol provides a voice of strength and encouragement throughout this meticulously written book. Her advice is both practical and useful. Most importantly, she shares with us her own intuitive sense and inspires us to seek it for ourselves within.

In today's world we have so much information, and, at times, misinformation, at our fingertips, that it can become overwhelming. Being able to use our intuition to harness and cultivate the courage and wisdom within can be the best and most effective information that we can use. This book helps us trust in using it. Utilizing this approach will allow the information and treatment offered by the medical team to be as successful as possible.

Believing in and keeping a positive outlook on our comprehensive treatment plan is also crucial. Carol's story really explores and offers ways and ideas that can help improve our outlook and optimize our treatment plan. Ultimately, how we know, do, and survive a cancer diagnosis hinges on our outlook. Outlook inevitably relies on our support system. It is estimated that having a strong support system and positive outlook can improve our cancer survival outcome by up to 50%. Enriching and strengthening our own spiritual and social network is vital.

In all, this book helps to provide Carol's human story of survival with keen insight and practical advice that empowers and inspires all of us to trust, appreciate, and utilize our intuition. Overall, with grace and gratitude, this intuitive approach to healing is there to guide us in knowing, doing, and surviving a cancer diagnosis.

- Walid Faraj, DO, ABFM, ABIHM

Preface

If you are reading this book, chances are that you are currently facing cancer or perhaps another significant health challenge—if not you personally, then someone close to you. If *knowing, doing,* and *surviving* is your game plan, then allow me to inspire you to take the intuitive approach to healing so that you can also experience *The Empowered Cancer Journey.* (If not cancer, this book still applies.)

Throughout the book, you will learn much about my specific story. My intention is that you benefit from valuable information that came into my awareness along my path to healing from Stage III Metastatic Head and Neck Cancer. Take from this book that which feels right and know there is a subliminal prayer contained within these pages which asks the Divine to guide you and protect you always—and so it is!

Having an open heart and mind will enable you to more easily navigate through some of the chaos that sometimes ensues—especially upon initial diagnosis. I encourage you to calmly and intuitively strategize your own step-by-step process. Every person is a unique, energetic expression; each illness is also individual, and all of us are on a very different path. Having said that, we can still learn from each other regardless of these factors, and it is my intention to be a support for your very special journey—may this book serve as a helpful resource.

The "knowing" I refer to in the sub-title is the *obvious* and the *un-obvious*. It's *obvious* that if the illness is correctly diagnosed and medically understood that there is a better chance that it can be treated and hopefully overcome with the correct approach. The *unobvious* is that any illness must be understood and treated from all angles—the mind, the body, the emotions (I refer to these combined aspects as The Mindbody), and the Soul if you want to increase your chances of survival. Fully embracing life from a place of empowerment will enable you to make the correct choices for your health care as well as all other aspects of life, and it doesn't have to feel like a burden. Tuning into your *Inner Physician* (Spirit) and allowing that part of you to be the ultimate source of wisdom is the key. This is also known as "using your *intuition.*"

Although I urge you to not rely on others to decide for you, I am by no means implying that your doctors and other health care providers are not going to be an important part of your journey— they will provide the Science. However, the decisions about what actions to take and the timing of it all should come from Spirit, the part of you that is also quite aware of Science since it is *all-knowing*! I will remind you throughout the book to exercise your muscle of intuition, which means listening to the voice of your Higher Self. This will enable you to feel more secure with your decisions.

The "doing" part comes from following the guidance of your intuition speaking from that empowered place that lives within you with intention. I urge you to get in touch with the thoughts you think, the emotions that surface, the sensations within your body and its overall condition, and the lessons your Soul is striving to learn. Once you have that figured out, which is usually done in stages, you can take appropriate action, step by step (I always felt that my guidance was on a "need-to-know" basis). There are therapies and practices that can help you sort out the (mostly untrue) stories that your mind has been telling you, the impact that your "undigested emotions" have had on your level of well-being, the ways you can improve the functioning of your body through detoxification and proper nutrition, and finally what it is that your Soul is wanting to explore that will take you further on your path. All therapies and practices that raise your vibrational frequency (yes, all things vibrate) will initiate a greater state of well-being, and that's the ticket called "surviving."

As difficult as it is to express this thought, it is necessary to say that surviving can mean to fully recover from the diagnosed illness, or it can mean to survive long enough for your Soul to learn the Spiritual lessons necessary for its fulfillment, which is why we incarnate into this glorious life. I know it's not an easy thing to ponder, so don't. Just live each day with a renewed commitment to keeping your mind and heart open and clear no matter how your fearful ego might try to sabotage the day.

It is healing to acknowledge all of the abundance with which you have been blessed and all of the people, places, and things that are making your journey the unique experience it is intended to be. I pray that your healing journey is a truly empowered one, one that is possible when utilizing your intuition every step of the way and taking action based on that higher wisdom.

Please Note: It was my intention to sequence the information contained within this book in a way that would be most useful to the reader. I do hope you receive the insights as you need them.

Namaste
(I honor the Higher Power that is you).

Disclaimer: This book is in no way intended to offer medical advice. Anyone diagnosed with a serious illness should be under the care of a trained medical team (multiple eyes on you). My only suggestion is that you choose your practitioners carefully and be certain that those you do choose are as good at listening as they are with dispensing their advice. Always check in with your Intuitive Self to confirm that you are in alignment with their perspective. And if you're thinking to yourself that you have never been in tune with your Intuition, remember it is like a muscle: the more you trust that inner voice, the more it develops.

*I dedicate this book to my spiritual brother
and guide, Sean, my beautiful, talented, and inspiring friend,
Celeste Yarnall, Bill, who allowed me to help him find peace
before passing over to the other side and then to ensure his wife,
Vicki, that he was in a good place, and the countless others that
have crossed over after bravely enduring the challenges
associated with serious illness.*

Chapter 1
OMG, I Have Cancer!

O n the morning of January 7, 2015, my life changed in a moment. It actually felt as if it had become someone else's life, not my own. As I lay on the biopsy table at a local clinic, I knew things weren't going well. While I was being probed and prodded, the energy around me felt a lot like frustration. Perhaps it was the sighs coming from the pathologist that provided my first clue that this procedure wasn't working out as planned. I asked her what was happening and why so many needles were being inserted into my neck (I think I had already counted 17 pokes). She told me that she had not been able to retrieve enough cells to test because of the high volume of localized blood, which was all that she was capturing. As those words left her lips, I felt my body become stiff while my brain began to race at 150 miles per hour.

Before walking through the clinic door, my thought had been that the Ear, Nose and Throat specialist (ENT) that prescribed the biopsy of my swollen lymph node on the left side of my neck would feel foolish once he received the results. I was convinced that my angry-looking throat was nothing more than inflamed tonsils due to trapped particles called "tonsil stones," and that the swollen node was just my body's way of processing the debris. I

1

felt that I was wasting time being at that clinic, especially since I had a job interview that morning and would have preferred spending the time preparing for it. But, after hearing the pathologist's response to my inquiry about all of the neck pokes, my brain immediately computed that an increased blood supply to an area could mean only one thing: new blood vessels were created (*angiogenesis*) to feed a growing tumor. My brain exploded with "OMG, I have cancer!"

After the 18th or 19th poke, the doctor stepped away from the table and said she thought she had finally retrieved a sufficient amount of cells and headed into her small lab. Her assistant stood by as I lay numb on the table unable to move even though I wanted to get up and scream. Within a few minutes the pathologist emerged from her lab and gave me the good news: it wasn't lymphoma. She assured me I would receive a call from the ENT by the next day since the tissue samples had to be sent to a lab endowed with more sophisticated equipment to determine the type of cancer growing in my throat and neck.

I managed to compose myself enough to roll onto my side and slide off the table. With weakened knees, I carefully landed on my feet. I gazed out of the window of that tiny clinic noticing that everything looked strange... the trees, the sky, even the cars in the parking lot. My very loud thoughts were telling me that everything had changed and my life would be very different from that moment forward. It was the most surreal experience of my life thus far. "Cancer happens to other people, not me; not organic, little ol` me."

With every good intention, the pathologist and her assistant assured me that a cancer diagnosis wasn't necessarily a death sentence. Very matter-of-factly, they told me that with surgery, chemotherapy, and radiation, I could fight back. I quickly gathered my things and high-tailed out of that office. I thought to myself "Hell no, I will not subject my sick body to those insults in an effort to heal." My gut told me that the answers I needed were out there and I would have to rely on my computer, intuition, and God's grace.

Getting the Ball Rolling Immediately!

I called the spa owner from the parking lot and told her that something significant came up, so I would not be able to interview that morning. She must have heard the terror in my voice because she responded with kindness and told me to take care of myself, including that if I ever wished to apply in the future, I would be welcomed to do so.

I don't quite remember driving home, but when I found myself in the parking lot of my apartment building, I took a deep breath and told the part of me that was freaking out that I needed to pull it together. I realized it was going to be up to me, myself and I to figure this out, so I had to clear my head and put the overwhelm aside. When I finally got out of the car and went inside, I immediately started making a list of everyone I needed to call; my supervisor was on the top of that list

Because of how I approach things, I knew I needed to start medical leave that day so I could begin researching just exactly how I was going to overcome this dreaded illness. I decided that I was going to be the most important person in my life and that everything not related to my becoming well was going to have to wait or go away. My primary goal was to create a solid game plan, and since knowledge is power, I had to educate myself.

As the day progressed, I had moments of intense clarity and knew I was totally in the moment, but then I would drift off into unknown places within my head, trying to fully grasp what was happening. Simultaneously, I was mentally working to find sensible solutions. My brain was spinning in a repetitive pattern at times. I had to find a way to snap out of it, so I kept making calls; each time I said the news out loud, it sunk in a little deeper. Finally, I had called everyone on the list with the exception of my family. I have a small family, a son and daughter-in-law (who had just announced they were expecting their first child), a sister, a married niece, and some cousins. Since I was living in Orange County, CA (SoCal) and my son and his wife were in the San Francisco area, I decided I would drive up to see them rather than share this news over the phone, but the majority of my family was in New Jersey, so I would eventually have to call them. My niece was about to have a surgical procedure done, so I figured this news could wait until she was in the clear.

On that day, one of the important individuals I would have to reach out to was my insurance agent. I did not have health insurance at the time (only life insurance), and that was quite a scary thought. I had to decide on a plan that I could afford, and my agent had to get me enrolled as soon as possible. Thank goodness Obamacare allowed for someone like me to enroll with a pre-existing condition and have coverage by the following month. During the call, one important fact that Mike, my agent, brought to my attention was that I was covered by a life insurance policy that had a critical health rider, meaning that since I had been diagnosed with a life-threatening disease, I could collect on the face value of the policy. In that moment, I could have kissed him! This was very important to me because I knew that I would be choosing alternative protocols and nutritional products to improve my overall state of being, and I knew health insurance was not going to pay for that. But I also knew that securing health insurance *would* allow me to have the tests and scans that I would need along the way, making it valuable coverage to have.

The Official Diagnosis

It was the next day that I received the definitive diagnosis: Squamous Cell Carcinoma. When I received the call from the ENT, I asked what his treatment approach would be, and without even taking a breath, he said, "Surgery, chemo, and radiation." I told him that I didn't feel comfortable taking that route without exploring all of my options, and in response, he told me that I didn't need to contact his office again. Well, ok, he was clearly not going to be a part of my medical team, but I was rather shocked by his callous reaction. Then again, most mainstream physicians don't have a Plan B, and they don't understand when patients are not willing to immediately submit to the "Standard of Care" protocols without doing their "due diligence."

As an Esthetician (Skincare Specialist), I knew Squamous Cell Carcinoma was a skin cancer, but I didn't realize that it could grow on *any* epithelial tissue. I would later learn through the results of my first PET CT Scan that it was growing on my left palatine tonsil and had infiltrated into several lymph nodes on the left side of my neck. It was considered Stage III, which was startling to hear because the only thing I thought I knew about cancer at that point was that Stage IV usually meant a death sentence. Did this mean that I was only one stage away?

As I researched more and more, I came to learn that people *do* survive Stage IV, so I was relieved and even more convinced that I was going to overcome this condition. Aside from that realization, I couldn't help but notice the irony that I had developed a cancer that affected the very type of tissue that I had been professionally caring for over three decades.

The Most Important Conversation

Although overwhelmed with thought, I suddenly stopped dead in my tracks and realized I hadn't really spoken with God beyond saying His name out loud in the parking lot the previous day. I had contacted key people to get things rolling, but now I needed to connect with my Creator, the only One that absolutely knew what I needed in this situation, including why this was occurring. I asked Him to bring all of the "beings" (people and spirits), places, and things into my awareness that would ultimately take me into the "end zone." My heart and mind were open to receive guidance like never before. In the past, it was for basic day-to-day challenges, but this was a big nut to crack, and I was committed to paying attention at a whole new level.

In the most profound way, I knew that I was truly heard, and I felt in every cell of my being that I would be ok, regardless of the outcome. In hindsight, I realize that this was the most important conversation I would have with myself during the course of my healing. I had set the foundation for future dialoguing, which would be important in moments to come when I would feel scared, confused, or alone.

Chapter 2
Strengthening Your Intuitive Muscle

N ow that I have shared my initial experience with you, I would like to articulate one of the most important concepts that will make the difference between you going through this experience as a patient being treated for a disease or an "empowered partner on your path to healing." If you are in tune with your Mindbody through exercising your intuitive muscle (which anyone can do), you will make wise choices. Remember that you are your own best physician. Your body's innate wisdom will surpass any other source of insight, so I have outlined the correct tools you need to fully access that information and feel confident that you are making correct choices from that place of knowing. It is, of course, important to check in with the professionals that you chose as your health care practitioners. As part of my daily prayers, I always remembered to ask The Divine to infuse them all with higher wisdom so that they could have the insight they needed to oversee my care. When you're all on the same page, you'll know that all are divinely inspired.

The following techniques have helped me strengthen my intuitive muscle, and they can also help you.

What to Ask

We can sometimes become mentally "scrambled" when trying to get a handle on our health. Besides there being so many unanswered questions within your own mind, people will try to influence your process (with good intention) by throwing a lot of (unknowingly) fear-based "what ifs" your way.

If possible, sit down, breathe, and get clear about precisely what information you need in the moment, and then write down the question(s) you'll need to ask to unravel that information.

Consider your words carefully so as not to confuse The Universal Data Base (which is the source of wisdom that will provide you with the answers you are seeking). Think about it in the same way as when you're trying to access information on the internet: if you don't choose the correct keywords that precisely reflect the information you are trying to obtain, you will find yourself sifting through a plethora of websites, blogs, articles, etc. Eventually you learn to narrow it down by posing the right question or using specific words or phrases; the same principle applies here.

How to Ask

Once you have identified the question(s), try one of the following techniques:

Prayer. Go directly to the Source and ask for an answer to your question or concern (either aloud or in your mind). Be patient for the answer, but don't be afraid to ask for a specific way to receive that answer. (I'll explain more about how to listen below.)

Meditation. There are so many different ways to meditate. I like focusing on a point, and for me that is usually behind my eyes. I use my breath to quiet my mind—deep, slow breaths work best for me. When I feel a greater sense of peace, I then raise my focus from that chosen point upward and shift it towards the back of my head. I request that I be shown what I need to know in the moment, or I pose the exact question for which I need an answer. Again, I ask to be shown in a specific way (see "How to Listen). Another method of meditation that works well is "Guided Meditation." This does require someone taking you on a mini-journey of self-exploration, but answers often emerge, sometimes immediately, either in the form of a metaphor or directly.

Have a conversation with yourself. For example, talk to a body part that needs attention. Tell it that you're giving it the opportunity to say what it needs to say and ask it to speak in a language that you will understand. Wait for a response. This might be a bit more advanced, but if you do this consistently, it just may be the best tool for you. Our cells are wired for communication; it's only a matter of understanding the language.

How to Listen

Your Mindbody Intelligence wants you to efficiently receive the information you are requesting. The following techniques are tried and true. Not trusting your Mindbody Intelligence is a huge obstacle to overcome, but with time, you will become more relaxed, especially as you begin to experience results.

Muscle testing (Applied Kinesiology) responses are a great avenue of expression that your body uses which will enable you to obtain answers. The question requires a "yes" or a "no" answer. Your muscles will go strong with a "yes" and weak with a "no." This includes testing a product by placing it into your energy field. Mostly this requires the assistance of someone else, but there is a "pulling apart of the finger" technique that I never mastered. A variation of this is getting grounded and centered (while standing), and then holding a product or object that you wish to test into your chest and asking "yes" or "no." If your body gently sways forward, it's a "yes," and if the response is "no," you will gently sway backwards. This is your Inner Physician letting you know what it wants and needs.

Asking for signs and synchronicities to come into your awareness is yet another way to obtain answers. Wikipedia has Carl Jung's version of synchronicity; it's worth a read. If you ask a question, suggest that a particular sign (numbers, songs, books, movie titles, colors, etc.) will clearly "show up." I know this may sound "hokey," but it works if you learn to tune in to these signs. A good example might be that a particular treatment for which you were scheduled (that you're on the fence about) cannot take place because the machine broke down... you understand what I'm saying! Synchronicities also occur to give you the confirmation that you desire. Example: crossing paths with a person who (without prompting) shares the information you are seeking, especially when you least expect to see or hear from this individual. Information that seems to come "out of the blue" should be explored if it seems to potentially pertain to you. You may find some great pearls of wisdom. God will speak to you in various ways!!!!

Body Sensations (somatic observations) are an easy way to know if you're on the right track with an answer. If something is right for you, your physical gut will speak to you. It's also possible that you will feel the truth elsewhere in your body, maybe in your head (may feel less burdened), your lower back (may feel unrestricted from the Universal Support), or even your legs can feel lighter (making it easier to take action). I always go with my gut because it speaks volumes, especially when I encounter something/someone that is not my best choice. I tend to obtain a great sense of peace all over when something/someone is the best option (in that time and space).

When I am faced with complicated decisions, I sometimes use "automatic writing" to give my unconscious a chance to speak in another way. I clear my mind and heart, pick up a pad and a pen, write the questions (in order of importance), and let it rip! Sometimes it can take a while before you get to the right answer, but you will feel it. I tend to cry when I experience profound truth, but that's just me. Your Higher Self may have another way of giving you that experience.

Last but not least: dreams. I pay attention to my dreams—always. Some will be more telling than others. There are times when your greatest fears or issues that have created an anger response in your body may play out through your dreams. Other emotions that you have not fully processed may also create scenarios that are experienced in the dream state. Other times your dreams will reach deep into your Soul for the answers you need to improve your state of well-being. My (deceased) mother once told me in a dream that I needed to get back to my Yoga practice; she was absolutely correct and she shared that information just at the right time! My mom also offered guidance when I launched my essential oil line. It's best to write down your dreams when you first awaken so as not to forget them. There are professionals that are skilled in dream interpretation to help you if you have one that really nudges you, but you can't quite understand all of the implications. Most dreams speak to you in metaphors, but not always.

Receiving Confirmation

I always ask for confirmation: Three things which occur that assure me that I'm receiving and understanding the information correctly. It could be the combination of a sign, a synchronicity, a dream, a feeling in my body or muscle testing responses. Intelligence knows that I need to feel confident in my decision-making process and so it will oblige!

Other tools you may consider might be astrology, numerology, or a psychic reading by a reputable psychic. The psychic sciences may not be for everyone, and by all means, don't read something out of the newspaper and think that it applies to you. A specific astrology or numerology chart based on your birthdate, the time, and the location of where you were born (and so on) are significant. A true psychic will come to you through a recommendation; don't pick one off the internet unless you feel that you've been spiritually guided to a particular individual—remember the 3-way confirmation.

We all have been blessed with intuition, some more than others, quite in the same way that some folks have leaner, stronger bodies without even trying and others have to work hard to achieve that level of fitness and muscular strength. The bottom line is that we all can improve our intuitive muscle.

Work consistently towards strengthening your ability to tune into your spiritual guidance and increase your willingness to live from that empowered state of being. Stay committed, learn to trust, and ask for confirmation.

Chapter 3
The Medical Machine

Over the next several months, I googled relentlessly to find any and all things cancer-related, including alternative cancer centers, doctors, and organizations, as well as informational websites that offered results-oriented diet suggestions, supplements (designed to support the body in various ways during serious illness), and alternative, safe science-based methods that were reportedly working for many people. I researched the Rick Simpson cannabis protocol and tried to get on board with it. Obtaining a medical marijuana card was fairly easy in California, and I was able to buy high-quality cannabis in oil form, which I put under my tongue for maximum absorption potential. But since I was pretty much on my own, being stoned out of my head most of the day was not serving me, so it's safe to say that the effects were more than I could handle; I had to discontinue this protocol. If I had a "care-taker," perhaps I would have continued since the benefits of cannabis are phenomenal. In Chapter 7, however, I do mention that I reintroduced cannabis into my routine in the form of vaping (which was milder) as opposed to putting the strong oil under my tongue. It did later serve an important purpose.

After considering the massive amount of information I had collected from various sources, my original thoughts had become louder than ever: I didn't want to be a product of the "Medical Machine" without trying more natural, less-invasive therapies. I guess I really knew which way I was leaning from the conversation I had with the ENT that had delivered the official diagnosis. I decided that I would try as many alternative therapies that I could afford – those of which, of course, resonated with me.

I have never been much of a fan of typical Western medicine, which I refer to as "mainstream". I watched my mother's health deteriorate over the years as she ingested bottles of pharmaceutical drugs. Despite the fact that she was diabetic, she was not consistently inspired by her physicians to eat healthy and to exercise. And when my mom developed pain in her lower back, I told her Internist that I felt strongly that this pain was her kidneys trying to speak out. I came to this conclusion after providing my mom with several sessions of body work. Her doctors completely dismissed my assessment, but my mother ultimately died of kidney failure. As intuitive as she was, I wished Mom had used her gift of insight to take a more proactive role in her health care. Rather, she hung on the words of her physicians; her family did not have much impact on her decision-making process and I believe she was too fearful to listen to her intuition.

I'm not even sure if I made up the term "Medical Machine" or if I heard it somewhere and fully realized its implications. Wikipedia states that a machine is a mechanical structure that uses power to apply forces and control movement to perform an intended action. From my perspective, the following entities make up the medical "mechanical structure" which try to have control over patient care: Big Pharma (pharmaceutical companies that produce prescription drugs), mainstream physicians who are directly and indirectly trained by Big Pharma, the good ol' FDA (Food and Drug Administration) who is clearly "in bed" with Big Pharma, and hospitals and companies that produce medical equipment used in treating cancer patients or those with life-threatening diseases. Combined they are a powerful force with an intended action: to sell products (drugs) and services that make lots of money.

Keep in mind how much money has been spent to prevent and cure cancer, yet the number of people diagnosed keeps increasing while the survival rate has not really increased as much as one would hope considering all of the billions of dollars spent.

When a person receives a diagnosis of a life-threatening illness, the first reaction to the news is generally fear, which is then typically followed by confusion. The mind races and all thoughts and emotional responses seem to blend into one another. This process can continue for days. So, it is easy to understand how impossible it could be for someone in that position to make sound decisions around having their health restored. This is where the wheels of "The Medical Machine" begin to turn.

Before a patient could even begin to think about potential options that exist to overcome his or her illness, the medical strategy has already been designed. Patients assume that "doctors know best," so they prepare for their journey into the unknown with a false sense of security. Most patients are too overwhelmed to take the initiative to research their disease and find alternative or even complementary methods. In the case of cancer, patients too often sign up for the "cut, burn, and poison" Standard of Care Protocol without question.

If the FDA truly placed the welfare of ill people first, they would not approve drugs produced by Big Pharma that typically provide low benefit and high risk. The effectiveness requirement for a drug to be approved by the FDA is very low, especially when it comes to chemotherapy drugs, although the expense for these drugs is over the top. CNBC reported that spending on cancer medicines totaled $107 billion worldwide in 2015 and is projected to exceed $150 billion by 2020, reflecting adoption of newer, pricier therapies, according to a report from the IMS Institute for Healthcare Informatics.

Because most medical research is funded by Big Pharma, their power has infiltrated the entire medical field. And truth is coming to light regarding the inter-connectedness between Big Pharma and the FDA. Check out medshadow.org. It reports, "An eye-opening investigation published last week by Science Magazine found that many doctors and researchers who sat on committees (for the FDA) for drugs that were approved then received significant kickbacks from the pharmaceutical companies behind those medications."

Another website to check out is in-training.org. Here's an excerpt from an article entitled "The Pharmaceutical Industry's Role in U.S. Medical Education," written by Rijul Kshirsagar and Priscilla Vu, found on that site which I also found interesting:

> As medical students are increasingly subjected to pharmaceutical marketing throughout their education, their skepticism towards the practices of the pharmaceutical industry gradually diminishes. Multiple studies report a relationship between exposure to the pharmaceutical industry and positive attitudes about industry interactions. As students' exposure to the

pharmaceutical industry increases, their ability to determine industry bias decreases. In losing their ability to detect bias and analyze pharmaceutical marketing statements objectively, medical students hinder their future ability to practice evidence-based medicine.

Now, let's consider surgery and radiation therapy. You can only imagine how incredibly expensive medical equipment is for hospitals and other surgery centers. These medical facilities must recoup their money by making sure their machines are in use as often as possible. It might be interesting to read an article by Dr. Robert Pearl, Stanford University professor and bestselling author of "Mistreated: Why We Think We're Getting Good Health Care—And Why We're Usually Wrong." Here's an excerpt from that article:

> But when doctors and hospitals make large capital investments in their own medical equipment, even well-meaning professionals tend to favor approaches that benefit their bottom line.

Please understand that I am not trying to imply that doctors who invested a lot of time and money into their education have only one motivating factor when it comes to prescribing therapies for their patients, but the pressure and influence to keep "The Medical Machine" rolling must be enormous.

But there's more to consider. The major food companies (Monsanto and the like) use fillers, chemicals, and genetically modified ingredients in their products that make people ill. Mainstream physicians, with the help of Big Pharma and the FDA, then come to the rescue and treat these ills with other harmful substances which in turn create more illness.

Having said that, I do believe that some medication is helpful at times, when prescribed in the correct dosage and for the correct length of time, but our consumption of drugs is excessive. My question is this: Is this whole process of getting ill a conspiracy? Each one of these entities is making a significant profit while society is becoming more and more ill. Imagine the fallout if suddenly we all started to educate ourselves in regard to eating well and using natural cures when indicated, rather than eating chemical-infused dead food that makes us ill, and then consuming harmful chemicals in an effort to get better. I think this "Medical Machine" as we know it would crumble, but we would become a more empowered and healthier society.

Before moving on, I would just like to mention that while I was seeking support from organizations, The American Cancer Society could not help me since I was not undergoing the Standard of Care Protocol; they follow a strict policy. It was so timely when the very next day I received an email from them (not sure on which list my name appeared) and they were asking for a financial donation. That's the day I told my friends on Facebook about my diagnosis, because I had to let off some steam about the long-reaching stronghold approach of The Medical Machine.

Mainstream Doctors: Think Outside the Box

It's interesting how the treatment outcomes are often entirely different from what a doctor presumes it will be, but they keep making medical recommendations based on the same textbook-directed protocols and "well-researched" prescription drugs offered by Big Pharma.

Without looking at the whole person, mainstream doctors are shooting in the dark. They try one thing, then another, and then another; this is where I believe the term "medical practice" originated! Do we really want them "practicing" on us when our lives are at stake?

Unless our mainstream physicians start thinking outside of the box, they will proceed within their practice wearing blinders and falling short of providing the best possible care to their patients. The information about alternative or adjunct therapies and modalities is available to them, just as it is to us, but physicians have to stretch themselves beyond mediocrity, choose to be better educated, and consider treating from a holistic perspective.

As I previously mentioned, the problem that lies within the existing mainstream model (aside from physicians being brain-washed) is that conventional physicians do not look at the whole person (patient) and his or her individual states of being when prescribing treatment protocols. For the most part, they often assume that it's a "one size fits all" game with few variations. But there are actually many variables - many unseen/un-known factors related to each patient that physicians just don't take into account. That is why there are so many errors made in medicine. The current approach is unrealistic to say the least. If physicians would realize that we are each unique individuals in all aspects (physically, emotionally, and on a Soul level), they may start helping the masses, one person at a time.

Our overall tissue/organ health, our physical and emotional scars (which could prevent energy flow), our unique physiology, and most importantly, our frame of mind have to all be taken into consideration. I suppose expecting a physician to take the Soul's journey into account is asking too much, so we do need other guidance to make us whole. That's where our own intuition comes into play. We and our doctors should be "partners" in the business of getting and keeping ourselves as well as we can be.

Chapter 4
Assembling My A-Team
–Choosing Wisely

During my preliminary research phase which lasted for about two months, I consulted with physicians and non-physicians before I started to assemble my team. I sought out practitioners specialized in a holistic approach to healing cancer and other significant illnesses. Some were those I had found on the internet, and others were found through people that I knew, but I just wasn't finding a good fit. I wasn't convinced that I had met anyone that saw me for who I am, nor did they offer anything that truly resonated with me, until I found Dr. A.

While searching for a Nutritionist, I came upon a chiropractor that offered a video on his website that truly grabbed my attention. In this video presentation, he talked about Bio-Cranial Release Technique, and I was intrigued. I scheduled an appointment and subsequently met with Dr. James Augustine in La Palma, CA. Most people I spoke with, including my family, could not understand why I would choose a chiropractor as my first health care practitioner, but nonetheless, I proceeded.

My treatment course with Dr. A was rigorous, thorough, and precisely targeted. I underwent a few tests to determine the overall condition of my body systems, and Heart Variability was one of them. Oh boy, oh boy; it was determined that I was a hot mess! My autonomic nervous system was completely out of balance, my digestion was shot to hell, my immunity was in the toilet (no surprise there), and if I remember correctly, my circulation wasn't all that terrific either. I immediately thought, "Where do we even start?" But, of course, Dr. A was already configuring a game plan and things were about to get real.

Instinctively, I knew that my cells needed increased energy if I wanted to survive, so I signed up for a series of PEMF (Pulsed Electro Magnetic Frequency) treatments that promised to increase ATP (Adenosine Triphosphate), which is a high-energy molecule found in every cell. Additionally, by having regular Bio-Cranial adjustments, we were resetting my autonomic nervous system so my body would actually have a chance to heal and not constantly be in overdrive; what a concept!

Dr. A and I worked as a team to create an all-inclusive program to build my cellular health. We continuously used muscle-testing (applied kinesiology) to keep checking in with my Inner Physician to be sure of which supplements I needed. Periodically, we would change the combination of nutrients I would need to take   based on muscle testing confirmation. I was confident that I was getting exactly what I needed, when I needed it.

As my internal self was being physically healed through nutrition and simple detox protocols (mostly infra-red sauna exposure), emotional purging inevitably began to occur. I experienced mood swings, going from elation to depression, and all places in between. My Mindbody was trying to keep up with all of the changes that were occurring at a cellular level. It started to become a chicken/egg situation, as the cells began to release debris, my emotions were stirred up. By the same token, as my emotions were finally coming up to the surface, the physical aspect of my being was shifting in response. It was a total party; yep, it felt a little like insanity and Dr. A was privileged enough to witness all of this craziness! However, it wasn't until a bit further into the process that I started to get to the core of my emotional state of being.

Expanding My Team

At this point, my intuition was telling me it was time to get another perspective, so finding a medical doctor that I could trust was the next order of business; I knew it wasn't going to be easy. The previous physicians with whom I had consulted either wanted to completely run the show by insisting that I be treated with a plethora of high-cost alternative protocols and products, or they wanted to move forward with mainstream Standard of Care methods; neither of these strategies were resonating with me. But then, by the grace of God, "I found gold," and this new professional partnership would help me get to the next level.

I first became aware of Dr. Walid Faraj, Doctor of Osteopathy, during a search on the internet. Initially, I was guided to a website while looking for a gynecologist. After I knew I would schedule with Dr. Mitchell for my yearly exam, I continued to read the bios of other physicians and practitioners working at TLC (Tustin Longevity Center). It seemed as if Dr. Faraj's good energy was somehow emitted through my monitor's screen and what I read about him was instantly resonating. I acknowledged the immediate sense of peace and comfort that I was feeling and I knew I needed to connect with him. Consequently, during my appointment with Dr. Mitchell later that week and without mentioning my intention, she recommended that I should consult with Dr. Faraj. Ok, confirmed! I concluded that I was about to sign up another Team Player!

While I sat in Dr. Faraj's office for our first consultation, I found myself talking a mile a minute. We had a wonderful exchange, each sharing knowledge and information as it related to increasing my overall health and he suggested which tests would be necessary to further understand what my body needed. I shared with him what I had done thus far and he was pleased that continuing with good nutrition and high-quality supplements were high on my list of priorities. Besides ordering blood work, Dr. Faraj felt it was necessary to also order a Chelation Challenge to determine if I had heavy metals in my body. Since I'm prone to having high levels of intestinal Candida (yeast), I had learned that it's important to rid the body of any mercury. * So, as thorough as I am, I was definitely down for the test. Having high levels of lead, mercury or any of the other undesirable metals can really take its toll on the body's immune system.

At the end of our first visit, Dr. Faraj expressed that his patients often become overwhelmed by the amount of information he would share, but in this case (as he took copious notes), he said he found himself in the opposite chair; he was overwhelmed by the amount of information I shared regarding what I had learned, what I was already doing/practicing and what I felt was important that I accomplish to help me increase my state of health. With that said, the most important thing Dr. Faraj told me during this initial consultation was that he honored my intuition. That was it for me! I certainly had found a partner that was prepared to help me reach the next level of health without ego and with an understanding of the importance of having a connection to Source (God).

Throughout the entire process, Dr. Faraj was helping to guide my Mindbody with science, but in a holistic way, and that's exactly what I needed; I knew that intuitively. He did, however, make it very clear that he was not treating the cancer and that I needed to find an oncologist as soon as possible.

* "The Candida Mercury Connection" by Kellyann Andrews includes a quote from Dr. Mark Sircus. He says, "Mercury-fed Candida becomes more and more virulent and eventually penetrates the intestinal walls and invades the cells. These fungal microorganisms become quite at home in the cell, and can easily be considered a principle characteristic of cancer." For more information, visit https://www.platinumenergysystems.ca/the-candida-mercury-connection/

Reinforcements

During this time of picking and choosing professionals that I could trust and that would help me get to the finish line (yes, there were times when I lost sight of the fact that the journey is just as important as the end result), there was another amazing health care provider that was already in my corner, helping in various capacities. Dr. Cathy Wong, DC, with whom I had worked for several years as an esthetician and body work practitioner, was keeping me in adjustment and had been instrumental in helping me put together cold laser protocols as an adjunct treatment that I could do on my own, even before the diagnosis. As per her recommendation, I chose to purchase a cold laser base unit. I began using the unit to balance my Chakras (energy centers), to provide ATP (energy) to my cells, to help stay grounded and relaxed, and to release cellular memory that was not serving my highest good. I later purchased The Lotus and introduced the violet laser into my auric field for a more in-depth clearing of emotional debris.

Dr. Cathy very generously provided many, many sessions of an uncommon style of chiropractic adjustment known as DNFT (Directional Non-Force Technique), which is offered by very few doctors around the country. Her ability to accurately muscle test to find the areas that needed to be adjusted has always been "right on."

I was aware of the concept of only having specific vertebrae or segments adjusted that needed to be placed back into alignment and not necessarily the entire spine if it was not indicated. Having the spine aligned is so crucial to the functioning of the entire body. When our vertebrae are out of alignment, nerves that link to our organs or other body parts can become impinged which could potentially cause a subluxation (a decrease the functioning of the corresponding organ, gland, or muscle controlled by that nerve), and I seriously didn't want any of those. With a simple, non-invasive thumb press, Dr. Cathy was able to realign the vertebrae that needed attention.

In addition, the style of muscle testing that Dr. Cathy provides was also very accurate when it came to choosing nutritional supplements or checking for food/substance allergies. Cross-referencing the outcomes of muscle testing performed by Dr. A and Dr. Cathy always kept me on track, and they were always in sync!

Aligning with Acupuncture

I have always responded well to Acupuncture for a variety of conditions, mostly pain, but for other random health concerns as well. I knew that I wanted to add this modality to my list of alternative treatments right from the beginning, but choosing the right practitioner was another story! After consulting with a few licensed acupuncturists, I found Kristin Hauser in Costa Mesa.

When I came under her care, I was emotionally unglued due to some family issues. Kristin was a great listener and allowed me to think out loud (and to some degree "unload") before every session. I believe this made the difference with how well I responded to the session. My experiences were profound while on her treatment table; very often, I gained mental clarity, and other times, I felt my body shifting into an improved state of being. I knew that opening up the energetic pathways so organ systems could function more efficiently was a really important component. Although the cancer was limited to the head and neck region, when one area of the body is affected by disease or dysfunction, the whole body gets the memo! If you want a strong Mindbody, all of you must be treated to maintain balance (homeostasis). Acupuncture is being accepted more and more by mainstream medicine because its benefits cannot be denied.

Additional Support

You will always be your own best source of comfort and support if you embrace your innate power and strength that originates from The Divine. Having said that, I suggest allowing others to come into your inner circle who understands what you may be dealing with and are prepared to be good listeners rather than offer unsolicited advice. This group could consist of individuals who previously struggled with a serious illness or perhaps were a support for another friend or family member during a time of crisis.

Besides sharing your day-to-day experiences and concerns with them, allow your support team to nudge you back to the most positive state of being all along the way. If you are faced with people that cannot offer that type of support to you and instead try to host a pity party, they just won't do! Remember this is all about you keeping your vibrational frequency as high as possible. Having negative thoughts in your "auric field" will sabotage that goal.

Trust that the Universe will send you the right people, but also remember that we are always challenged to "keep it real." Not everyone is operating at the highest frequency and discernment is required. The more you are around positive-minded people, the more you will immediately recognize when someone is not the best support for you.

Your inner circle could be comprised of friends, physicians/other health care practitioners, acquaintances, friends of friends, or even those you have served in the past. We are all interconnected and each person that comes into our life plays a different role. But I do urge you to keep checking in to see who serves your Higher Purpose. Some may come into our life to help us learn more about who we are at the core by *not* being in alignment with our truth; this can serve the purpose of keeping us strong and authentic, but remember it's better to surround ourselves with those that *are* in alignment with who we are at the core as much as possible.

One of the first people that I called upon receiving the diagnosis was an acquaintance who works within the medical field. After the initial phone conversation, she came to visit, and as we sat in my small-but-quaint studio apartment, she began to describe her experience in the operating room where she worked as a surgical nurse. I felt myself becoming more and more anxious as she described a neck dissection procedure. She continued by sharing her experience with chemotherapy patients and finally the effects of radiation that she witnessed. The walls started to feel as if they were closing in on me until I finally blurted out that for those reasons, I was not taking that so-called "healing" path. Immediately, a look of confusion came over her face as she proceeded to ask me why I wasn't going to sign up for the "Standard of Care" protocol. My response seemed to irritate her when I clearly stated that I knew there was a better way for me to handle this illness if I wanted to fully recover with minimum side effects. In response, she told me that I was being irresponsible because I had a grandson on the way.

Subsequently, other attempts were made via email to get me on board with what she thought was my best chance for survival, but I had to stand up for myself; I had to let her know that I could only welcome people into my support circle that did not judge my decisions regardless of their personal opinions.

Had I succumbed to her pressure, I don't believe I would have survived. I am not suggesting that her advice was ill-intended by any means, but when I stated that I had to listen to my guidance and sort out all of the information that I was gathering, she could not comprehend what I was saying. Unfortunately, once she left my apartment, our relationship was over.

Most people in my life knew that I had to be the one to live (or not live) with my decisions. I would never want anyone to be put in a position of choosing for me and making the wrong choice. Also, if others make decisions for you, you will find it difficult to ever feel empowered in any situation.

It pays to do your own research and observe what information is actually resonating with you and what is not. Remember that if you're a well-adjusted, in-tune person, ultimately you are the "authority" regarding your own health and well-being. You chose your team of professionals for a reason, but always be a part of the process of finding the best physical, emotional and spiritual food that will heal you in all of those aspects.

Chapter 5
Taking Care of Self

I acknowledge that I am so very fortunate to attract all of what I need (when I need it) to assist me in small ways and large ways. My heart could just explode with gratitude for everything/everyone that shows up in a timely manner when I'm open to receiving and living in the present.

If I had fallen into a mode of victimhood, denial, or fatalistic thinking during the illness, none of the right folks or tools would have made a difference, so I urge you, once again, to open your mind and your heart and let it all in. Choose to embrace what you're going through and let life happen, even when we don't always know the why. I always say I'm on a "need-to-know basis," and that's the truth. All things are eventually revealed, we just have to keep our eye on the ball and follow our gut. With a positive outlook and trust in Source, you too will find yourself attracting all the right resources that will help you travel down your path with greater ease.

Below I have outlined some of the self-care practices that I either sought out or that fell onto my path. I do believe that approaching disease from all angles is crucial. Consistency is important and a certain level of discipline, just remember that you are so worth the effort!

Improving Circulation

I realized the importance of keeping my blood flowing optimally on a regular basis so that my cells could be nourished and oxygenated more efficiently. Bringing fresh blood through my capillaries would improve my body's overall healing and strengthening capabilities, and I knew that had to be a part of my usual routine. Having been introduced to a PEMF device by Dr. A, I knew I would have to continue with an at-home device since I responded so well to the sixteen consecutive sessions I received at the office.

As one could imagine, there are strict FDA guidelines regarding claims made about devices, so I'm not at liberty to give a brand name, but I can share my experiences with you.

Where do I begin? Well, I felt stronger than I suspected I would feel and my Emotional Body went through periods of "dislodging" trapped emotional debris from my tissues. One of the most significant experiences occurred one morning when I awakened to a state of extreme anxiety and confusion. I knew I was not feeling like myself which was unfortunate since I was scheduled to get together with my friend, Vicki, in a few hours. I called to tell her that I just couldn't pull it together, but when she heard the sound of my voice, she said she was coming right over.

There are a lot of healers and healing apparatuses in this world and California seems to either create them or attract many of them across her borders. With that said,

Vicki got on the phone with a healer friend in San Diego and asked her to "work on me" remotely. Together, with clear intention, they began to clear my energy field and send in a higher vibration. By the time Vicki reached my door, the angst had greatly diminished. "What a great tandem effect," I thought. "This PEMF device initiated a process that would enable me to release trapped stress from my cells and then allow me to feel the support of people who are capable of and willing to reach out with their special, Divinely-inspired gifts."

Once I worked through the emotionally-charged debris, I felt like a million bucks! I went on with my day and felt even better the next morning. God bless the healers in whatever form they appear.

Nutritional Requirements: The Ever-Changing Scenario

I just can't stress enough the importance of good nutrition, including choosing the correct supplements. The various ones that I took to build my body were almost all chosen via muscle testing. Others, especially the ones recommended by Dr. Faraj, were chosen based on results of blood work, so I was changing and replacing as needed.

When one is not eating enough food, supplements play a very important role in achieving health and wellness. The fruits and vegetables that we eat unfortunately don't contain the same high levels of nutrients that were once enjoyed by our parents and grandparents. Organic produce is always the best choice when possible and there are various fruits and veggies that I would never eat unless they were organic: berries, leafy greens, or anything without a thick skin (which protects it from pesticides) to be specific. It's more expensive at the check-out line, but hell,

I'm worth it and you are too! I could get a bit more in-depth about eating organic, but there's much information on the internet and in books that you can read about. If you have access to locally-grown, organic produce, that's always your best choice.

Juice Plus+® supplements were built into my daily routine. They were chosen because they come from real food and there's a ton of research behind them to substantiate all of their claims. I had wanted to choose the gummies over the capsules because I had so many capsules to swallow, but there is a certain amount of natural sugar (although low) in the gummies while none in the capsules. Since I was trying to consume only 20-40 grams of carbs per day, I figured I'd rather save my ration of carbs for foods, so I opted to take the capsules. I had peace of mind knowing that although I wasn't eating large amounts of food, I was still getting the nutrients my cells needed.

It's important to be consistent with all that you're doing for the purpose of healing, but taking your supplements at the right time is crucial, so I want to share an organizing tip: Set the alarm on your cell phone or any device that allows you to set multiple alerts. My phone alarm was set to go off almost hourly since I was taking so many formulas that had to be taken at different times of the day, either away from food or other supplements. If you truly want to get the most from your investment (time and money), you must have a system in place. Yes, my life felt rather regimented, but it's safe to say that it paid off. (Read "More About the Needs of the Body" below for additional nutritional information).

CranioSacral Therapy

I would like to share a style of body work, CranioSacral Therapy (CST), which was instrumental in helping me become better prepared to cope with the disease and ultimately allowed me to release debris stored in my Mindbody. The insight and sense of empowerment I gained from having multiple sessions cannot be downplayed and, in the paragraphs, below, you will understand more.

CST releases restrictions in the fascia that prevent proper functioning of the CranioSacral System, which is comprised of the membranes and cerebrospinal fluid that surround and protect the brain and spinal cord. Undigested emotions often weave into the fascia and create discord and dysfunction. When we have restrictions in our fascia (the protective membrane just under the skin) we can feel out-of-sorts on many, if not all, levels.

When I received the diagnosis, my reason for scheduling a CST session was to explore the reasons why I had created this in my body. To some of you, the concept that we create our own cancer may be foreign, if not ridiculous-sounding, but none-the-less, it's true to some extent. As explained in other chapters, our emotions can affect our health if not processed correctly and completely. But what I didn't mention earlier is that we can inherit (into our DNA) undigested emotions from our ancestors. Yep! It's true and I'll tell you a quick story about my "ancestral visitation," and no, I'm not crazy!

While lying on my therapist's (Rachelle) table during my first session of CST after receiving the diagnosis, she was energetically brought to my neck region. I had not shared with her where the cancer was located, only that I had recently received the news. She felt a lot of heat building up in that area and as she shared that with me, I saw the face of a woman in my mind's eye—larger than life. Her hair was up in a stylish bun, she appeared to be approximately forty-five years of age and she was beautiful—soft and seemingly docile. It appeared that she lived during the 1800s. She proceeded to tell me that the women in my mother's lineage were oppressed and not able to speak their truth or share their pain, and I was chosen, in this lifetime, to break that cycle. I was stunned at what I was seeing and hearing in my head. "Could this be real?"

As I shared this brief experience with Rachelle, she said she could feel the heat in my neck spontaneously dissipate. It was as if the message had been delivered, so I could now start this journey of discovery and healing.

I had never learned about any of my ancestors except my grandmother (mom's mom), who had died before I was born. There was some mention of oppression and even cruelty that existed in her life and even in my mother's younger years. Sicilian men, especially back in the day, could be very dominating and perhaps a bit insensitive. What I know is that my grandfather could not tolerate the moans and cries that resulted from my grandmother's pain while she struggled with breast cancer. He would insist that she be quiet, and my mother ached for her.

After my grandmother passed, my mom was not treated with the kindness that a young woman who lost her mom deserved. She found her voice in later years, but the damage was already done. I believe it never completely healed; thus, it was passed along via her DNA to me. Oddly enough, from the time I was a small child, I had recurring tonsillitis and upper respiratory illnesses. Throat and heart chakra issues which relate to expressing emotional pain.

After giving it some thought, it did seem to make sense. I have been known to be very "vocal", so who better than me to break the cycle of verbal oppression? Although, verbalizing in excess could be as detrimental as not speaking up, I guess I was destined to learn and eventually address all issues concerned with "The Avenue of Expression." Read more on CST in Chapter 11.

More About the Needs of the Body

During my research I had learned that certain processes needed to occur for me to become as healthy as I wanted to be and I have mentioned some of them, but here's a more comprehensive outline:

1. **Detoxification** through infrared sauna, Ozone Therapy (a medical blood purification method), Chelation Therapy through medical IV method, Modified Citrus Pectin with algae and brown seaweed (both excellent for removing heavy metals), Gold Roast organic coffee enemas (reduces toxins in the bowel and liver if done properly), and sensible exercise so that I could sweat out some impurities while keeping my muscles (including my heart) as healthy and strong as possible. It is important to find protocols and techniques to remove the cellular and extra-cellular debris so that your cells can begin moving

towards a state of health, rather than moving towards destruction.

2. **Increased nutrition** through eating a variety of organic, healthy foods, including superfoods like raw cacao, quinoa, blueberries, garlic, avocado, kale, broccoli, chia and hemp seeds), raw juices (not everyone does well with all varieties of juice, so listen to your body), and oral supplements. Antioxidants are particularly important since they are designed to fight cellar damage due to free radicals. You may wish to consider medical Vitamin C IVs and a medicinal mushroom formula (high in beta glucans) from Host Defense called My Community. Additionally, I incorporated supplements designed to activate the "natural killer cells" that fight cancer. It was also recommended that I take a systemic enzyme called Vitalzyme XE to digest the biofilm that surrounds and protects tumors, giving my immune system a fighting chance to find the cancer cells and obliterate them. Vitamin D3 is advised for everyone because of its many benefits, including balancing insulin and blood pressure, and because of its ability to turn off cancer-causing genes while turning on immune-protecting genes.

3. **Oxygenation** through deep breathing exercises and perhaps the use of a PEMF device.

4. **Decreasing inflammation** via eating a low carb diet, eating ginger and taking Turmeric (curcumin) and/or

bromelain. Check proper dosing with your nutritional counselor.

5.   **Building cellular energy** through nutrition and devices that impact the mitochondria, like PEMF.

6.   **Cancer-starving** through avoiding sugar and limiting carb intake to 20-40 grams per day. Forget the pasta, bread, rice (except black rice in small amounts), pizza, donuts, pancakes, muffins, candy (except chocolate made with organic cacao and no sugar—Sinless Raw Chocolate was my choice), and definitely alcoholic beverages should be avoided completely.

7.   **Stress reduction** via prayer, meditation (including Chakra clearing and rebalancing), correct deep breathing exercises, yoga, affirmations, CranioSacral Therapy, reflexology, aromatherapy (or any other body work modality that resonates with you), sensible exercise, and most importantly, being around uplifting/highly vibrating human beings.

8.   **Paying attention to oral bacteria** and other pathogens stemming from the teeth and gums, because if they get into the bloodstream, they can make one ill. Be sure you have that covered!

9.   **Staying alkaline** through drinking alkaline water, avoiding over-consumption of acidic foods, and eating a lot of greens... I was introduced to alkaline water years ago and have been drinking it ever since. I learned that

pathogens don't grow in an alkaline environment, so we have to keep neutralizing the acidity that occurs in the body for a variety of reasons, including over-consumption of acidic foods and beverages (meat, most dairy, grains, sugar, certain fruits, processed foods and alcohol), stress and lack of exercise as well as too much exercise. Eating a lot of greens is also helpful because the green element, chlorophyll, is one of the most alkaline substances we can consume. There are many acid/alkaline charts available online to get a full list and plan your diet accordingly.

10. **Avoiding harmful electro-magnetic fields** when possible (Wi-Fi, microwave ovens, etc.)

It's All a Process—Rome Wasn't Built in a Day!

Try not to become overwhelmed with implementing all of the necessary components required to achieving improved health all at once. Stressing yourself will be counterproductive. Take steps to move in the right direction by incorporating the easiest steps (that have not already been part of your daily practice) first with consistency, but not with stress-producing urgency. Get it done, but pace yourself. Most of all, allow your intuition to choose the correct products and practices that best suit you and your needs. You will find that your needs will change at different phases of the illness so stay in tune with your Mindbody.

If you believe that we are all here for a reason, then allow your life to unfold as it's intended. I believe we incarnate to this planet with the purpose of elevating our consciousness and experiencing life with a greater sense of awareness, which brings greater joy. To that end, we choose the lessons that must be learned so that we can overcome living the ego-based life and rise to the level of heart-centered living. The Universe creates the circumstances that allow that to happen if we are open to the experience.

I, for one, am still learning and growing and will inevitably make mistakes as part of the process, but one thing that's really important to realize is that living without awareness is not really living it's more or less struggling to exist. Each day we have to choose to settle our brain and let our Spirit step forward. This can occur when we meditate and there are many approaches to reaching this state of suspended thinking where the brain surrenders and the Soul's will can impart its wisdom into your conscious and unconscious mind. Our Higher Mind takes over when we adjust the functioning of the brain and allow it only to relay information coming in from Source to the conscious and unconscious mind.

Eckart Tolle says that we tend to live in the past or the future without taking the time to appreciate the present moment. I think it's fair to say that often times that is how we miss the guidance that is available to us. And trust me, I do realize how difficult it can be breathing into the present experience; we are so programmed to recall the past so as to not remake mistakes or to live in the future in an effort to create a more secure one. But, living in the moment prevents us from feeling stress—try it. Prevent your mind from drifting back in time or projecting forward and you will be delighted at how liberating the present truly is.

Choosing to redesign our daily process of making decisions requires practice, some discipline and total honesty with ourselves. Our decisions are often clouded by old thinking patterns and the opinions of others because we haven't fully embraced the concept of intuitively obtaining the information we need to make those very important decisions. Get clear! We should examine each thought that is taking us towards our decisions... Are they emotionally based? Are they our thoughts or someone else's? Have we asked for guidance? What are we feeling in our gut?

To expand upon my decision-making process described in Chapter 2......I often begin by centering myself (a form of meditation that involves aligning our Energy Centers known as the Charkas). I breath into being as present as I can be (to my level of awareness and ability). I treat the issue at hand as if it's the first time I'm faced with it (without bias). I push out any ideas that pop into my head that don't resonate with me. I decide if I have all the information I need to make the decision. If I feel I need to, I research more until my intuition tells me I'm ready to decide and then I do! Whether you start with asking for the best choice to surface intuitively or you end with that (after doing all the steps above), it doesn't really matter as long as, in the end, the decision feels good in your body. I suggest not making any decisions too quickly; follow the process you choose to get to the truth.

Exploring Other Factors

Our overall state of health is most often a choice. Just because we are genetically predisposed to a specific condition does not mean we will necessarily develop that condition, or if we do, we often can decide (consciously or unconsciously) to what extent we will experience that condition or disease and how we feel overall.

Epigenetics matter more than genetics. What we eat, where we live, when/how we sleep, how we exercise—all of these can eventually cause chemical modifications around our genes and enable them to turn on or off over time. (See www.whatisepigenetics.com). I'm certain by now you have realized that our emotions, including the trapped ones, can be added to the list of epigenetic factors that can also impact our health.

It is important to note that when we're stressed from emotional overload or if we find ourselves frequently in the "fight-or-flight" mode, our adrenal glands produce cortisol to help us manage the stress. This is an important function, but when we're frequently in that state, the high levels of cortisol circulating through our body can create health issues such as weight gain, high blood pressure, muscle weakness, mood swings, improper thyroid function, fluctuating blood sugar levels, poor sleeping patterns, low immunity and impaired brain function. Once our cortisol levels are depleted (a condition referred to as "adrenal burnout"), we are at risk for equally-troubling health issues, including rapid weight loss, fatigue, heart palpitations and immune dysfunction.

Our endocrine system (which produces hormones) is responsible for regulating all of our other body systems, so keeping it balanced by managing our stress levels and by having regular blood work keeps us "in the know."

We have a choice: to live a healthy life or succumb to the effects of negative thinking/feeling/living. Having said that, there are cases of babies being born with illness, so what's my take on that? I believe we are born into the life we choose while still living in the Spirit World. I don't have all of the answers, but I do believe that as Spirits or incarnations of Spirit, we have power beyond what we realize, the power to place ourselves in circumstances that have an impact on our own lives and the lives of others.

The Custom-Fit Approach

When it comes to choosing your physical protocols, it's often a "weeding process." Among the plethora of diets, supplements, mainstream medical protocols, and alternative treatments, you will find what is right for you. Remember that "you are you" and not anyone else. What sometimes works for others might not be the best course of action for you, but it doesn't have to be complicated. State your intention to make the best choices, ask questions, listen to your team of experts, check in with yourself and decide.

<u>To sum it up:</u>
Inner Guidance + Professional Advice (from reliable sources) + Positive Action = Positive Outcome. *Knowing, Doing, Surviving*

Regarding emotional well-being, there are various methods (discussed later) that can assist you in achieving and maintaining your emotional health. Under normal circumstances, we are constantly challenged to face our emotions, process them and move on. But, when we're dealing with (sometimes) life-threatening issues, our emotions can start to control us; try not to let that happen. I know it's "easier said than done," so if you need help with processing and keeping the balance, get the help you need.

Since having a serious illness is often a life-changing experience, we often tend to consider our spiritual life more than ever. Do we have one? Do we want one? Do we need one? Well, thus far, you've done a lot of reading on the subject as I described the processes I used on my cancer journey, so I think it's safe to say that without a belief and reliance on something greater than your ego-self, I believe it may be a rougher road. I will not say that it's impossible to survive an illness unless you believe in a version of "God," but when the source of guidance is limited to the rational mind, in my opinion, one is working with limited resources. I know in my heart that without the higher "knowing" and the guided "doing," "surviving" would have been an insurmountable challenge for me.

Staying Connected

You have to be prepared to walk this journey with one foot in front of the other, on your terms, and based on the knowledge you have of your Mindbody. I encourage you to strive to be your best advocate, your best researcher and realize that you are the only one who can truly feel what your body needs. Always keep your mind and heart connected to your Innate Wisdom. If you believe in God and I sure as hell hope you do, He and his cohorts will be the ones to guide, protect and enlighten you, be it directly or through other people (yes, including your open-minded, tuned-in health care providers). I know I have constantly repeated the concept of tuning in to guidance, I just cannot stress enough the impact it had on my life and on my journey.

We have a whole team of Higher Beings in our corner at all times, all we have to do is ask for direction and protection. In Chapter 7, I share my personal experience with the "heavy hitters"—Spiritual Beings that I called in for extra healing and protection when I needed it most. When I intuitively decided I was fully ready physically and emotionally to take the next step, I wanted them by my side to be extensions of my own power and to provide the comfort that I knew I would need. I chose to not only accept human support where I found it, but also, in accordance with my birth right, I accepted the collaboration of all the Avatars, Angels, Spirit Guides and Ancestors whose power, knowledge and wisdom worked through me, for me and sometimes in lieu of me.

Spend Your Energy Wisely

It is wise to use all of your energy for the things that will bring you closer to being healthy. Once you come to terms with what is actually happening in your life, it is best to leave judgments, frustration, doubt and fear in the far distance. It's tempting to have pity parties and sometimes you might, but let those parties end before they really get started. I cannot stress enough how important it is to relinquish any negative thoughts and feeling that may come upon you as quickly as possible. Your cells will respond favorably to gratitude, peace, and calmness, and you will have an easier time if you embrace the importance of finding ways to elevate your Spirit; I know you can do that.

There will be the occasion when you feel other people's sympathy; don't buy into it. You have a strong Spirit which is sometimes buried under the emotions based in fear, but nonetheless, it's your greatest resource. People generally mean well and they want you to know that they care, but they may not realize how their own fear could impact you. I found myself reassuring people along the way that it was going to be ok, whatever the outcome. Each time I expressed my strength, it made me even stronger.

Let's face it, there is no "how-to" book which outlines exactly how to walk this path, but just know that you make the rules, you set the pace and ultimately it's your perception that creates your reality.

During this time, you are at the center and everything and everyone is in the periphery. Reach for what you need when you need it and trust that it will be there if it's for your highest good. If for a moment you think it won't be, create what you are seeking in your mind's eye and watch what happens. God did not create you to leave you on your own. If you ever do feel alone because you find yourself in this unique situation, just know that it's a time-out to regroup and to get ready for the next step in your process, whatever that may be.

Love is all around you, and if you ask for love manifested as understanding, strength, and a sense of peace, you will receive that. Keeping your heart open is the key to becoming a better expression of divinity; that's the honest truth!

Trying to Keep Life Normal and Balanced

I had driven to San Francisco in March for my son's wedding ceremony at City Hall, accompanied by my sister. It was tiring driving almost 1,000 miles round trip, but I have always loved to drive, especially on the coast. I took my time, stopping along the way to rest and I finally decided I was very pleased that I made the effort.

The official wedding celebration, which would take place in Ohio, was the most important event that was coming up on the calendar (other than the birth of my grandson) and come hell or high water, I was going! However, I knew it would be a bit trickier traveling the distance alone while being further along in the cancer process. It would require sound planning and execution, but as my mother always said, "Where there's a will, there's a way." I will never forget her words, so I flew to Ohio and attended the beautiful celebration. I ate clean, stayed on my supplement regiment, visited with relatives and friends, danced like no one else danced and made it back home safe and sound. Determination can take you a long way and that's how you win the game.

I was fortunate to be living in Orange County, so I went to the beach as often as I could. The negative ions that come off the salt water are so healthy for our Mindbody, and the sound/vision of the waves mesmerized me while transporting me to a place of calm reflection. Watching the sun set helped me to release and let go of any stress that may have crept in during the day. Breathing, watching, smelling, feeling, and appreciating, whether at the beach, in the mountains, or when walking in the woods, is more healing than you may imagine. Connecting with Mother Nature is not only an opportunity to enliven our senses, but a way to raise our vibrational frequency. Illness has a low frequency, so by elevating our frequency we are neutralizing the power of the illness.

Balancing the rational mind with the creative self is what allows you to move through your day with greater ease and less resistance. There were times when I would find myself obsessing about what I was or was not doing to help the cause. Then I would shift my perspective and ask if I was in alignment with my intuition. Most often, I was right where I was supposed to be, but when I wasn't, I would take a deep breath, still my mind and open my heart. Remember: in a state of calm is where you find truth.

Simple Techniques to Employ

There is a plethora of simple things we can do to create better Mindbody health, some of which I've already mentioned. Aromatherapy (as a stand-alone treatment via inhalation or application), meditation, reciting positive affirmations and mantras, prayer, conscious breathing, reading or listening to uplifting books, writing down all that we are grateful for in a journal, practicing Yoga, and receiving body work modalities are great choices. Include the ones that resonate with you, especially if they include the use of certain healing tools that enhance the benefits of any treatment, including semi-precious stones, crystals, aromatherapy, scalar wave cold laser, singing bowls and new age music. Also consider investing in a PEMF device to increase the functioning of your circulatory system and providing more cell energy.

Remember that surrounding ourselves with positive-minded people can lift our spirits (elevate our frequency), energize us physically and give us hope for a brighter future. As it is said, "Misery loves company." Avoid the pitfalls of buying into negative talk. It doesn't mean you cannot be a friend to someone who often discusses problems or who has a negative perspective on things, it just means that if you want to survive, you either have to remind them that positive thoughts bring around positive outcomes, or limit your time with them. When they leave, don't internalize any of "the bad vibes," but rather clear the low vibrations from your auric field by "smudging" the environment. To do this, safely burn white sage or Palo Santo wood sticks. There are smudging kits available online that you can purchase if you choose.

Chapter 6
Getting to the Core of Undigested Emotions

"In reaction to THOUGHT,
We experience EMOTION.
All emotions stem from
LOVE or FEAR.
Thoughts of LOVE bring forth HARMONY and BALANCE.
Fearful thoughts bring forth IMBALANCE.
Regarding HEALTH,
These disturbances
Are first realized by our SOUL.
It is our PHYSICAL BODY that ultimately manifests the
symptoms.
If our aim is to completely HEAL,
We must do so in our
MINDBODY and SOUL with guidance from SPIRIT."
-Carol L Fouad

I have worked within the beauty and wellness industry for over three decades. It is because of this direct contact with people that I came to understand how emotions affect us on a physical level, either immediately or over time. It seems that some folks are gifted when it comes to identifying how they feel in a situation, clearly expressing it to the right person (with empathy), then moving on without any significant residue remaining. But others may sometimes not be capable of either identifying the emotions they are experiencing in relationship to an occurrence, or they choose to not address them. I would like to share a portion of my life story so you could gain some insight into the negative outcomes of accumulating versus processing emotions based in fear. I refer to this as "harboring emotions." Please understand that the information below is not coming from a place of "victimhood," but rather from a place of "if only I knew then what I know now!"

Reflecting Back in Time for Growth and Understanding

I was told (and somewhat remember) that at age three, I would wake up, wash up, and dress myself. I would prepare and eat a simple breakfast, then go outside and play before my mother would arise. By the age of five, I could write the alphabet in cursive, tie my shoes and tell time (before digital clocks existed). It seems that I was born onto the Earth plane with the tendency towards "survival," which I would obviously need later in life.

I distinctly remember hearing a particular phrase over and over while I was quite young that was a common one in that era:

Children should be seen and not heard. Being a rather sensitive child, that phrase had an impact on me; I would often bury my feelings, but then, being human, I would act out when the pressure would build within.

My integrated neighborhood comprised of many cultures: mostly Italian, Polish, Irish, Puerto Rican, African American, and Cuban. This was not always easy. There was not the consistent cohesion that would come from understanding each other's differences, especially living under the conditions in which most of us lived: economic challenge. There was quite a lot of anger and fear in the community. Many of the teenagers that were drinking and taking drugs while hanging around the streets at all hours of the day and night made it sometimes feel unsafe, so we always had to watch our backs, even as small children.

For much of my childhood up into my teens, I was my mother's caretaker when she was ill, which seemed often. By the time I was nine years of age, I was skilled at preparing dinner for the family and completing other household tasks that most nine-year-olds seldom are required to do. In retrospect, it seemed as if I was continually being groomed for later years when it would be particularly necessary to know how to care for myself and be up for the task of getting myself through the tough times of my life. However, the truth of the matter was that my "Inner Child" was not receiving the age-appropriate nurturing that I needed during those tender years.

I did try to learn various self-soothing techniques while enduring six years of Catholic school. I taught myself not to cry when the nuns humiliated me through scolding, spanking, and having me parade from classroom to classroom with gum on my nose when I was caught chewing it. You see, I was self-conscious of my nose because I felt it was quite prominent (in later years I would have rhinoplasty and septoplasty which enabled me to feel better about myself). I wonder if that would have been as important to me if I had not been subjected to that method of discipline which encouraged the sense of feeling imperfect.

I finally convinced my mom to allow me to transfer to a public school where teachers seemed better adjusted in comparison to the nuns that often seemed angry. I do believe I became a slightly happier little girl.

From as far back as I can remember, I struggled with respiratory issues including walking pneumonia (twice) and several upper respiratory infections. In later years, I came to realize that the energy center related to the heart, chest, respiration and upper back (the Heart Chakra) were reflecting the emotions I was unable to process or effectively express. My tonsils were always inflamed; I remember having tonsillitis a few times each year. I believe my throat was holding on to the pain I could not articulate.

But, as I grew older into my teen years, it had become quite difficult for my parents to enforce any rules that conflicted with my developing belief system. I had been sponging all of the fear-based emotions that flooded our household and community, and as someone that always felt the need to be in survival mode in this unsteady environment, I took complete control of my life and decided it was best to live by my own rules. Although I wasn't developing emotionally, I felt like I was an adult, but this would come back to "bite me" in later years.

Then, before I knew it, I was married at the age of 20 and a mother by the following year. In a case of "insult added to injury," I found myself, once again, in a household riddled with fear-based energy rather than a home of marital bliss. There was jealousy, anger, disappointment, sadness, lack of trust and more anger. As a result, I developed asthma and then a serious lung infection that sent me to the hospital. All the while, my Inner Child was watching and waiting as my Heart Chakra was absorbing all of this energy without knowing how to release it and how to honor myself enough to stop the madness.

I struggled to be a wife while feeling unappreciated at best. I was dealing with the dichotomy of being someone who had the experience of being efficient and responsible as well as being the hurt little girl that just wanted to rebel against everything. I had a difficult time feeling and expressing love. As a mother, I didn't know how to relax and enjoy the gift I was given; I was so ungrounded by this time in my life that I lacked the ability to nurture my son in the way that he needed. I wish I could go back in time and "show up" as an emotionally healthy human being. I believe my relationship with my son would have been more solid through the years had I been a more patient and compassionate parent on a more consistent basis especially during his young and fragile years.

I divorced when my son was about three years of age, but I went on to be married two additional times over the next few decades. All marriages were a struggle and then there were none! I had sought professional help during a few phases of my life, but we never reached the core of the pain that had found a home in my Mindbody. Combining family dysfunction, abusive relationships (mostly mentally/emotionally), and the inability to share my thoughts and feelings in what I perceived to be a "safe" environment, I found myself among the "walking wounded." "If I only knew then what I know now," I may have done many things very differently. I suppose I decided early in life that everything was supposed to be a struggle because that's what I saw around me. But then, of course, there's the perspective that everything happens for a reason. I do believe I chose these challenges for the growth of my Soul, but the pain was real and I was not finding "avenues of expression" or a way to channel the negative energy.

Victimhood

When we allow unhealthy relationships or situations to continue occurring while having the power to change them (unknowingly in most cases) or remove them from our reality, we are operating from a place of victimhood mentality. It doesn't mean we aren't smart or that we want to suffer (then again - sometimes we think we deserve it), but mostly we are just afraid of the unknown, and we get comfortable with the familiar, whether on a conscious or unconscious level. We just go along with what we have come to believe is normal until something major causes us to stand up and smell the coffee; that usually does happen at some point in our life, but the question is, "Are we aware enough to recognize it when it does occur and then take action?"

It is not intended for us to be in pain, but when we are disconnected from Source and living without awareness, we struggle to a degree that seems beyond manageable. Since we are co-creators of our reality, we can manifest just about anything we choose in the form of pleasant or unpleasant experiences and circumstances. We tend to follow the patterns that are in place, but I came to realize that we can remove those patterns that keep us "stuck."

The "Pain Body"

There is actually a term that defines the accumulation of painful life experiences that were not fully processed in the moments they occurred, leaving behind an "energetic pattern". It is referred to as the "Pain Body," and it develops over time as we keep accumulating similar energy patterns from other painful experiences that we did not process. After some years, it emerges as an "energy entity."

Negative thought patterns vibrate at a lower frequency in comparison to positive thoughts patterns. Since emotions (which are also vibrations) occur in response to thoughts, the more negative the thoughts, the more negative the emotions.

A Pain Body becomes a physical disease or some level of dysfunction if the right type of energy clearing does not occur since our cells are damaged by fear-based, low-vibrating emotions. This process has been scientifically proven by Dr. Candace Pert, PhD—Johns Hopkins University (author of "Molecule of Emotions"). This is what we know to be true.

Physiological Changes Due to Emotions

The limbic system is the seat of our emotions, motivation, learning and memory. It has been scientifically established that the limbic system extends beyond the structures of the brain, contrary to what was previously believed. This system is part of "The Mindbody Super-Intelligence" that extends to each cell within our bodies. Undigested emotions can lodge in our cells within the fascia, organs and other tissues, which can lead to pain and dysfunction. This is how it works:

The Receptor: This protein molecule is found on the surface of cells in the body and brain. It responds to energy (vibration) and chemical cues by vibrating. It functions as a "scanner" waiting to pick up messages carried by other vibrating protein molecules. Let's consider the receptor to be like a "keyhole."

The Ligand: This is the message-carrying, vibrating protein molecule (emotional energy) that travels through interstitial fluid and binds to the receptor. Let's consider this to be the chemical "key" that fits into the keyhole.

The Receptor and the ligand vibrate together which forces the message through the cell membrane into the interior of the cell, causing a chain reaction of biochemical events. This can translate into physiological changes within the cells. Specific ligands fit into specific receptors.

The Receptors, believed by scientists to be part of our unconscious mind, accept and store information that has not been digested by our conscious mind. Any "negative" information (emotions that stem from fear) in the form of low vibrational frequencies can store in our cells and manifest into illness, while "positive" information (emotions/practices that stem from love) with a higher frequency can be absorbed by our cells and initiate a healing process.

The following is a list of emotions or states of being from Dr. David R. Hawkins' book, Power VS Force:

•Shame has an energy level of 20
•Guilt – level of 30
•Apathy – level of 50
•Grief – level of 75

- Fear – level of 100
- Desire – level of 125
- Anger – level of 150
- Pride – level of 175
- Courage – level of 200
- Neutrality – level of 250
- Willingness – level of 310
- Acceptance – level of 350
- Reason – level of 400
- Love – level of 500
- Joy – level of 540
- Peace – level of 600
- Enlightenment has an energy level of 700 – 1000

Putting the "Self-Saboteur" to Rest

I have learned to ask for protection from my Inner Saboteur, which still exists but is less active. When we're accustomed to things not going well (in any aspect of our life and according to our perspective), we sometimes sabotage success when it's within our reach. I do believe many of us embrace this archetype without realizing it. I can't say it's a subject I really delved into, but once I saw the patterns, I realized I was the only one that could change the outcomes of any given situation.

I now try to choose what is truly best for me in my life, and in doing so, it tends to also be good for the collective consciousness, since we're all connected energetically. I believe that my Higher Self chose the illness with which I was blessed so that I could find my way out of emotional pain and confusion and develop into a conscious, empowered individual. In doing so, I could perhaps help others dig deep for truth and healing. In addition, this was an opportunity to heal the generations of women that came before me in my maternal lineage.

Again, if we learn to live from our heart in the never-ending moment of now and clear negative impressions in our "attractor field," we can fully experience living from the place of our authentic power. All things become possible when we consciously live in accordance with the Law of Attraction, calling in what we truly desire rather than what we think we deserve, coming from a disempowered perspective.

Chapter 7
Amping it Up

After ten months of keeping up with a rigorous routine, I noticed that my overall health had greatly improved. I had incorporated the PEMF device, was using scalar wave laser programs, taking in all the wonderful supplements that my body needed, eating a very clean, sugar-free diet, exercising, doing gold-roast coffee enemas daily, and working on the emotional and spiritual parts of my being. However, my PET CT Scan showed that the cancer was still active in my tonsil and lymph nodes. Based on my interpretation of the report, the activity level had somewhat decreased, but the perimeters had not budged. I was hoping for better news, but I knew that I had not yet experienced all that was intended for this journey.

Hyperthermia and Radiation

I remember sitting at my computer ready to research more treatments, products, or anything else that might take me to the next level of health when I remembered reading about "hyperthermia." I learned that cancer cells cannot survive in temperatures at or above 107 degrees, so by heating the body to this intensity, the cancer cells die off. I also read that hyperthermia destroys the cancer stem cells. From what I understand, cancer stem cells, if not killed, can lie dormant just waiting to re-emerge and form new tumors.

I discovered that a local hospital offered hyperthermia. I was interested in the localized rather than the full-body treatment. I cannot imagine increasing the one's entire body temperature to over 107 degrees without serious repercussions.

I scheduled an appointment with a top radiology oncologist on staff at that local hospital and went in to see him for a consultation. I expressed my interest in hyperthermia and was informed that it was not an FDA stand-alone protocol; it had to be combined with either chemo or radiation. I inquired about low-dose radiation rather than the usual standard-of-care intensity and was told that it was not offered at their radiology unit.

I began to feel as if the doctor was using scare tactics to get me to sign the form to begin treatment. He told me my cancer was spreading into my sinuses and that I would not survive without radiation and/or chemotherapy. My gut told me to keep searching for other options, so I left the hospital and never returned.

I continued to research facilities that were offering hyperthermia and found a facility in Los Angeles. I scheduled a phone consultation followed by an in-person appointment after feeling that perhaps I had found what I was looking for. Before even going to the center, it was predetermined that my insurance would cover 100% of the treatments, but if they didn't, it was ok, because they accepted insurance assignment as full payment. I felt that, once again, I was directed to the people, places, and things that were the next to be experienced on my journey.

Within a few days, I drove up to LA and met with the staff. During my appointment, things started to progress very quickly, and before I knew it, I was being fitted for a radiation mask. I then found myself driving to Santa Monica to have the markings placed on the mask to ensure that the delivery of radiation would be precise.

"OMG, is this real?" I asked myself. "How did I get this far in one day? Am I really ready for this step?" I had previously thought that I would never consider having radiation "therapy" until I learned that the FDA approved hyperthermia only as an adjunct therapy to radiation (or chemo, which I would not agree to). The only way the insurance company would pay for treatment was if I was willing to have these therapies combined, so at this point, I really felt that I didn't have much of a choice. I knew in every cell of my being that hyperthermia was going to work for me, and I also knew that the low-dose radiation approach would be something I could survive. I saw it in my mind's eye that the cancer was not going to hold up to the heat bath or the damage to its DNA structure, and somehow, some way, I was going to come through it all very well.

Guides and Angels to the Rescue

At this point, I knew I had to assemble my Spirit Team, but it wasn't until I was on the radiation therapy table about to receive my first treatment when I (understandably) felt compelled to call in my special support and here's who showed up: Princess Diana (yes, I was a bit surprised!), Wilhelm Reich (an MD and psychoanalyst), along with three angels for protection. Princess Di offered me calmness, tranquility, and compassion, while Dr. Reich provided medical supervision and food for my rational mind. The angels had swords and I would later imagine that the radiation beams would bounce off of them, allowing only the beams that were actually going to destroy the cancer cells to reach my body—all others were deflected. This visualization helped to prevent fearful thoughts and to keep my mind's eye on the prize: complete elimination of any and all cancer cells and cancer stem cells.

Observing my breath, visualizing my support team at work, as well as releasing into the session is what got me through all of my radiation treatments (in addition to vaping cannabis to offset the nausea).

Hyperthermia was always a pleasant experience. The warmth generated from the machine, although directed only to my neck region, brought me comfort and I would generally fall asleep. I brought snacks and would reenergize myself before preparing to get back onto the highway heading home. My Soul, my mind, and my body would be nourished despite what had occurred on the radiation therapy table each day of treatment.

One of the mind-blowing aspects of receiving treatment was my ability to allow the technicians to snap my head into place (via the meshed mask) onto the table for treatment. The reason this surprised me was because I had been extremely claustrophobic for the better part of my adult life, ever since being trapped in an elevator while pregnant. It's amazing what a little Spiritual reinforcement can do to help us achieve our goal.

Chapter 8
Deciding It Was Over

Nine weeks of driving into LA five days a week in 405 traffic (for those of you who are familiar with this freeway that connects Orange County with LA, you get it!) was not an easy feat. I was ready to be done, but that was not the deciding factor that caused me to initially stop the radiation and hyperthermia treatments before completing the recommended protocol.

After receiving a "Body Talk" session (more in Chapter 11) with Marjorie Panzer in Newport Beach, I knew it was over. When I informed the cancer center that I would not be returning, that I was, in fact, cancer-free, they insisted that I sign papers stating that I was behaving irrationally, irresponsibly, and against doctor's orders by not completing the full protocol. I complied; but I knew what I knew!

In all honesty, I do sometimes have to sort out my "knowing" from my tendency towards stubbornness, being Sicilian, from New Jersey and born under the astrological sign of Leo with a Taurus rising, but as I describe what occurred, you may understand this decision.

I Flipped My Switch, Not My Lid

I distinctly know the very moment when my Mindbody "flipped the switch" from "cancer on" to "cancer off". I was in the middle of a Body Talk session and while Marjorie was connecting with an aspect of my being, I suddenly felt a major shift. It literally felt as if I had an internal light switch that was spontaneously repositioned and, in that moment, I felt a sense of peacefulness.

Well, perhaps it can be best described as a sense of peacefulness while simultaneously feeling an incredible sense of elation. Every cell in my body felt alive and surprisingly "unified and cohesive." I don't remember ever previously being aware of that overall sensation. I am certain there was that cellular alliance before specific cells rebelled, but it never came into my awareness like it did in that moment. I was certain that I was in an expedited state of overcoming the dysfunction that had ensued within my body for the last year.

After Marjorie had finished that segment of the session, which was executed quietly, she asked me if I had felt a change about ten minutes prior. I was so amazed that she was so in tune, because that was precisely when the shift occurred. I described my experience to her and she explained that there was a sudden change in my DNA structure, sort of the opposite of a mutation; the dysfunction reversed itself. I know that may seem impossible, but I am certain that is the very moment when my Mindbody decided it was over. Everything changed from that moment forward.

Tying Up Loose Ends

The cancer center had given me a two-month break before calling and insisting that I return for treatment. I told them that the cancer was no more and that it just didn't make sense to continue with a therapy that had potential dangers. Since they were persistent, I requested that they prescribe a PET CT Scan to prove what I knew to be true. They agreed and I immediately scheduled the tests at the usual imaging center in Santa Monica. Within a few days I was back on the scanner table, fully confident that I would be told there was no sign of cancer anywhere in my body.

I got onto the table enthusiastically and lay still as my body was slowly guided through the vessel. The previous weeks of lying on the radiation table flashed before me, and I was so ready for that experience to be a part of my past history.

As I sat waiting for the printed report and the images on CD, I started to create a new future for myself in my mind's eye. But, firstly, I knew that in the very near future, I seriously needed to eat something, since all that was offered at the imaging center were snacks that were loaded with sugar. If I learned anything during the entire cancer ordeal, it's that sugar is not our friend, it's our enemy.

I was determined to wait patiently, then celebrate with a fantastic lunch somewhere in LA! When the technician came out with my test results, I looked at her face and it was confirmed. Technicians are not allowed to provide official results, but her Soul spoke to me through her eyes and I was satisfied. I think I remember skipping out of the office, afterwards heading to a restaurant for some much-needed nourishment.

With love and gratitude in my heart and food in my belly, I headed straight back to the cancer center to deliver the test results and await the official report.

Having been blessed by God, guided by my Spirit team, and protected by my Angels, it was determined that I was, in fact, cancer-free. The staff at the center (once they lifted their jaws from the floor) was so excited, and needless to say, I was beyond elated! Once again, God had my back.

I stayed and chatted for a while and it was explained to me that historically there was a decreased chance of the cancer ever returning if I would undergo eight more very low dose sessions (a quarter of the already-low dose) of radiation along with the hyperthermia. The physicians and technicians could not give me a reason for this phenomenon, but they confirmed it was documented in the results, and they believed it in every fiber of their being. So, I agreed with their request; I would receive two sessions per week for four weeks to complete the protocol to their satisfaction.

I followed through with my commitment, and once I said my goodbyes and walked out of that door, I was so very ready to move forward from that experience as a new version of myself, complete with an unwavering faith in the power of God-connectedness, aka Intuition.

Chapter 9
What Just Happened?

It was March 23, 2016 when my Soul decided it was time to begin the emotional healing process associated with going through this health challenge. The first step of my process was fully acknowledging what had occurred and then getting in touch with my current state of being. I learned that in crisis, the mind, body, and Soul will do what's required to meet the challenges necessary to survive, if survival is the objective. In this case, the anguish was temporarily suppressed so that I could get through each day able to make decisions, care for my day-to-day needs and focus on a joyful future with my grandson, Evan. But, now that the eminent threat was over, it was time to begin releasing the energetic footprint of the accumulated emotions that had not been *fully* realized.

Guilt, anger, sadness, disbelief, confusion, and perhaps some fear, all related to this experience, seemed to surface at once. This process unexpectedly began to emerge while watching an episode of "Devious Maids." A female character was depicted having chemotherapy to treat bone cancer and suddenly the floodgates opened—yep, I lost it! I began to tremble, cry, shout, and walk around my living room in a circle like a crazy person.

My first shouted words were that of an apology to my body for exposing it to radiation. Rational or not, that's what was coming up from my deep unconscious. We're very complex beings, and although I did feel guided to make the decision to proceed with the low-dose radiation, there was a part of me that was saddened; I felt a sense of guilt that I enabled that assault on my Mindbody. "If my financial circumstances were different," I thought, "perhaps I would have shipped myself off to one of those expensive alternative cancer facilities." As that thought emerged, I felt anger bubbling up and wondered why we cannot choose the medical care we desire to help heal and sustain us. Thinking strictly in terms of Universal Oneness, shouldn't that type of holistic care be available to everyone, not only to those that are fortunate enough to have a sizeable bank account?

Rationalizing that we live in a capitalist society should have put things quickly in perspective, but when going through the first phase of emotional healing, rationale is often nowhere to be found! We generally begin this process from our lower selves (ego) until we can "create a clearing in the forest." Our vibrational frequency elevates as the density of our "lower" vibrating emotions diffuse. This can only happen if we are honest with how/what we feel. The sometimes less-than-obvious root cause (from old wounds) often becomes obvious at this time, but if it hasn't already, ask for insight.

I went on to my next thought: Will the side effects of the radiation (Xerostomia, low functioning salivary glands) be a constant reminder of the ordeal? If so, how will I manage the symptoms? All the little details emerged just as strongly as the bigger concerns; I just had to roll with it, so to speak.

The rants, now mostly in my head, went on to address family not showing up to support me in the way I had hoped and in accordance with my expectations (an example of the ego mind). I knew this would be a huge hurdle to overcome and it would take time for me to understand that aspect of my story. The truth of the matter is that I may never fully understand what occurred, since I made the mistake of writing a letter to each person concerned (letters that were generated from my ego rather than my heart), and in turn, a few family members have not spoken to me since.

I have often made the mistake in life of thinking that everyone thinks and feels the same way, but we know that's not the reality. People show up according to their ability to do so, and we cannot judge them based on their emotional limitations.

Another perspective is that people come into our life for a season and a reason to enable us and themselves to fulfill Spiritual contracts; that's the best way to look at situations that present a challenge. These contracts are made in Spirit and are fulfilled on the Earth-plane. However, sometimes I forget this and react to situations from a lower perspective, but I'm getting better at catching myself in the process.

Full Disclosure

My next thought I faced circled the confusion and disbelief associated with this: How does this happen to someone living a relatively healthy lifestyle?" However, I quickly came to the realization that although it was true that I was caring for my body with good food choices, exercise, and rest, I had unconsciously neglected the emotional aspect of who I was, and the unsettled mind and undigested emotions were begging for attention. The

Universe found a way to put them front and center, getting me to dig deep to the root cause of my Mindbody imbalance and become a much healthier version of myself after years of stowing away what I could not consciously face.

I eventually pulled myself together. I relaxed through breathing, had some tea, and knew that the next day would be a better day.

I shared this piece of my experience because we all need to see the humanness in each other. Yes, the Divine part is the most important, but by seeing and accepting what is or what was from the human perspective, we move closer to the Divine Self; life becomes easier because our mind is freer. However, I still strive to continuously rise above the ego; it's something we do for life.

Chapter 10
Thankfulness

I was brought to a state of non-cancer because of the beautiful synergy of all the modalities and disciplines I employed through guidance and perhaps also my insistence that I was going to survive. To sum it up: What you put into your body, your mind, and your Soul is what matters, regardless of where you are within these aspects when you start your journey. Having support on the good days and the not-so-good days is invaluable.

I would like to take this opportunity to acknowledge those that stood by me at different phases of my process, some even all along the way. Yes, it's a long list, but you will be blessed and inspired by reading it through.

First and foremost, I thank all the manifestations of The Divine that showed up whenever I called upon You (and even when I didn't). From Day 1 and all the way through my researching process, while I built my A-Team, whenever I had decisions to make (daily), during my more difficult treatment processes and then all the way to home plate, you were there. I continue to acknowledge your presence in my life each day (some days I'm more in tune than others) and appreciate that you neither judge nor laugh at me when I think, say, or do the weirdest things. Amen!

Jess (my son): I know you struggled through this experience on many levels, but I feel that through all that occurred, before, during, and after, we have come to a place of better understanding. I pray that our relationship continues to transform, providing us both with a greater sense of peace, love, and acceptance.

Evan (my grandson): In my heart of hearts, I have to say that both your anticipated and welcomed birth, three days before my birthday (what a gift!), is what kept me pushing along, and ultimately, you are the reason I chose to survive. You're Nana's little angel and always will be; we are Soul-fully connected. As I always say, "I love you to the moon and back." ❤

Lisa (my daughter-in-law): Thank you for giving us a beautiful baby boy. Things were tough, but we got through it.

Sherif and family: I appreciate your openheartedness and sincere concern for my well-being.

Kathy (my sister): I know it wasn't easy flying to Cali, but I think life provided us the opportunity to see the truth of our relationship.

Rosanne and Lou (my cousins): Thank you for checking in on me from so far away. Having family to rely on for support is important on any path.

Dr. A: Our deep conversations, your out-of-the-box tests, your knowledge, techniques, and protocols are what allowed me to realize the full scope of my condition and take proper action. You were my life-line; I'm truly grateful for your positive attitude about healing that helped me keep it together until I could see for myself that my body was growing stronger. I will be forever grateful for your presence in my life.

Dr. Faraj: I found gold when I found you and I knew that the very first time we met. You said that you honored my intuition and that made all the difference to me. We worked together as partners while making decisions about my medical care and this enabled me to feel empowered. Thank you for staying late in the office when I cried my eyes out for what seemed like hours. Your heart, your dedication, and your knowledge are what make you, you! And, of course, thank you to Linda and all the other amazing staff at TLC (Tustin Longevity Center).

Dr. Cathy: Your generosity, amazing knowledge and golden touch brought me enormous comfort. Thank you for your beautiful heart.

Lorrie, Virginia, and Peter: I will always remember your kindness when I needed extra support.

Kristin: Your empathic nature and knowledge of Acupuncture helped me to pull it together on days that weren't so terrific. Your understanding and inspiration took me a long way, maybe more than you realize.

Adrienne: Thank you for reaching out soon after I was diagnosed, it was so encouraging to speak with someone that made it through the cancer challenge by choosing the right guidance. I enjoyed our lunches and inspirational conversation.

Suki: Your friendship has meant more to me than you know. Thank you for your kindness and support all along the way.

Jenna (my lymph drainage practitioner): So happy I found you. Clearing the debris played a major role in assisting my body to heal.

Marjorie: I will never forget the moment I knew my DNA flipped its switch. Thank you for sharing your expertise as a Body Talk Practitioner. And Katie, your follow-up sessions of Body Talk helped me to keep digging for gold!

Fariba: Thank you for your Ayurvedic guidance and support. Your Marma Point Therapy sent me into La La Land!

Rachelle: Your insight and support were there from the beginning, when I needed it the most.

My East Coast friends, Diane, Kerry, Bill, Jody, Ro, and all of my Facebook family: Your encouragement and heartfelt care were more than appreciated. This all kept me going strong!

Ellie D: You brightened my days with flowers and lovely lunch dates. Thank you for reaching out and encouraging me along the way.

Marilyn S: Thank you for helping me to work through relationship issues and acknowledge my power and strength.

Dr. Osbourne: Although I did not become your patient, you supported what I knew to be true: that if I wanted to survive, I had to get my mind, body, and Soul in alignment and that was an impressive bit of wisdom coming from a "mainstream" physician.

Anonymous Supporter #1: I know it's preferred that your identity remains a secret, but my heart insists that my gratitude goes on record. When I didn't know how I would afford the crucial things I needed soon after the diagnosis, I reached out to you with a letter and you answered very generously. Your humanness, your kindness, and your willingness to help will provide you and your family with a lifetime of blessings.

Anonymous Supporter #2: I am not sure of your identity, but I do have my suspicions! Your gift enabled me to receive additional alternative care that was not covered by insurance and this gesture helped me to become stronger. Helping others at their greatest time of need immediately elevates your status, not only in my book, but in the Akashic Records!!!

My Spiritual brother Sean: Meeting you at the cancer center was a blessing as much as it was Divine intervention. Thank you for opening your heart and allowing me to share in your world, even for a short time. I know that you're doing big work now that you're operating from heaven and I will always think of you when I see a hummingbird, as you telepathically told me to do the night before you passed on to the other side. I know you're part of my current Spirit Team, watching over me and protecting me. It's a comfort knowing you're always a whisper away. I will always remember sharing our "special chocolate" and laughing senselessly while we tried to remember what we were talking about!

Celeste Yarnall: I admired your Leo Energy. The inspiration I received from you came from watching you in action. Your beauty, wisdom, and strength were unlike anything I had ever witnessed. You kept forging on throughout your entire cancer journey and stayed committed to your life's purpose until the very end.

I also want to acknowledge Lisa B, Whitney, Shannon, and Dina, a few of my loyal clients that proved just how blessed I am to be working within a field that gives me opportunities to connect with so many beautiful people with whom I share a special bond.

I'm grateful to the staff at the cancer center in Culver City (which is no longer in existence) who cared for me during my 9-weeks of therapy. That facility transformed my life in ways that one could never imagine.

And thank you to the various California-based physicians (primary MDs, oncologists, and ENTs) that stayed on top of my post-cancer throat health: Dr. Streeter (Santa Monica), Siddiqui (Vista), Jacobs (Oceanside), and Creamer (Newport Beach).

My dentists and their staff: Dr. Nichols (Huntington Beach), O'Reilly (Encinitas), Rockey (Newport Beach), Gashinsky, and

Vithlani (Millburn, NJ). Thank you for "putting out the fires" that were created during and after radiation therapy. I never realized how significant saliva production is to the health of our gums and teeth.

Last, but certainly not least, Serafina Angelina Trupia: Thank you, Mom, for comforting me from the Spirit world during times of anxiousness, especially when I was waiting for my second PET Scan, I smelled your scent. I will be forever grateful to you for teaching me how to be strong, persistent, and to have faith in our Creator. Until I see you again, keep on dancing in heaven with Dad.

People, places, and things that I needed appeared on my path, and I am so very thankful that I was tuned-in enough to acknowledge when the Divine was working on my behalf. Faith, trust, an openness to receive, and the commitment to keep moving forward is what healed me and that's what I wish and hope for you.

Release into Peace. ♥

Chapter 11
Resources & Information Guide

T he information provided below and throughout this book is intended to be used as a reference and is not to be followed in lieu of obtaining sound medical advice by qualified practitioners.

There are many resources for information online, as well as many modalities and treatments that may appear to offer the results that you're potentially looking for, but I urge you to choose with caution.

Below, I have outlined some resources for you to consider. Refer back to Chapter 5 to be sure you cover all your bases. Consider the physical, mental/emotional, and Spiritual aspects of who you are and proceed from there.

-*The Truth About Cancer* by Ty Bollinger

Cancer touches more lives than you may think. According to the World Health Organization, one out of three women alive today and one out of two men will face a cancer diagnosis in their lifetime. With the roll-out of "5G" that number may increase. To Ty Bollinger, this isn't just a statistic. It's personal. After losing seven members of his family to cancer over the course of a decade, Ty set out on a global quest to learn as much as he possibly could about cancer treatments and the medical industry that surrounds the disease. He has written this book to share what he's uncovered, some of which may shock you, and to give you new resources for coping with the cancer that is present in your life or in the life of someone you love. Visit thetruthaboutcancer.com for more info.

-The Micozzi Files, The Corbisin Cancer Secret and 55 More Covered-up Cures by Marc S. Micozzi, MD, Ph.D.

There is helpful information contained within this book – I recommend it.

-Body Talk

Body Talk is an integrative mind/body medicine which combines the Western and Eastern knowledge of neuroscience, anatomy and physiology principles of traditional Chinese medicine, acupuncture, yoga/meditation as well as philosophies, osteopathy, and energy psychology. The result is a non-invasive method to address many health problems that is safe for all ages. Testing the skin tension for a "yes" or "no" answer is often employed by the practitioner. Tapping is also used to implement the changes into the Mindbody. Visit https://www.bodytalksystem.com/practitioners/ to find a practitioner close to you.

Recommended Body Talk Practitioners:
Marjorie Panzer: http://integrated-wellness.com or call 949-673-8088.

Katie Holly: katiejoholly@me.com
(Both practitioners are available for one-on-one sessions
in Orange County, CA, or you may set up a remote
session at your convenience.)

-CranioSacral Therapy/Somato-Emotional Release

CST is a gentle, hands-on method of evaluating and enhancing
the functioning of a physiological body system called the craniosacral system, comprised of the membranes and cerebrospinal
fluid that surround and protect the brain and spinal cord. This
modality is excellent for any and all stress-related concerns. If
you're ready to get to the emotional root cause of your stress and
dysfunction, a trained CST Therapist using SER techniques can
delve into the information that your "Inner Physician" would like
to and is prepared to reveal. Visit Upledger.com to find a
Practitioner in your area.

-Foot Reflex-Aromatherapy℠

Reflex-Aromatherapy℠ is a combined approach of using a
specific aromatherapy formula designed to help process an
undigested emotion that has been revealed by The Inner
Physician along with the execution of a pressure-point technique
of the foot reflexes that correspond to the entire body. This
method is a wonderful anti-stress modality capable of creating a
sense of well-being through technique and the use of essential
oils known as "Vibrational Enhancement Formulas." Visit
corehealingessentials.com (my webpage) for more info.

-Consistent Meditation – Your Way

I just cannot stress enough the importance of clearing the Mindbody of the debris that we either pick up from our environment or create within our own being daily! At my website (www.corehealingessentials.com), there are some basic guided meditations to follow, but there are so many more out there that are very helpful.

My favorite evening meditation consists of breathing and releasing into a state of peace, enough so that I can begin using my creative visualization process. Starting at the First Chakra (root) and moving up through the Second (sacral) and Third Chakra (Solar Plexus), I envision releasing energy or debris that does not serve my higher purpose out through the bottoms of my feet through roots that connect to the core of the Earth. I then continue up to the Fourth Chakra (the heart/respiration) and release out through the breath. Moving up to the Fifth Chakra (throat), I allow myself the freedom of making sounds that express/release trapped energy connected to expression. I then move up to the Sixth Chakra (third eye) and release through my eyes, all that I saw either internally or externally. I am now ready to bring in the light through the Seventh Chakra (crown) that runs through my body, clearing any residual debris and bringing in Love from Source. It moves all the way through my body and down through the roots located at the bottoms of my feet and anchors into the core of the Earth. Next, I allow the grounding energy to move up through those same roots to bring stability and strength all the way up through the crown. Now, I enjoy feeling the energies mingle, each quite different, each creating a greater opportunity for healing and happiness.

-Diet (Please refer to Chapter 5)

Note: It's important to consistently have full panel blood work to remain aware of your body's changing nutritional needs. Please check with your Health Care Providers before taking any supplements or choosing any other methods of healing.

Just a side note, but an important one for anyone undergoing radiation therapy for Head & Neck Cancer: watermelon will be your best friend. When my tongue was filled with radiation burns, watermelon saved the day. I would take a bite of food (which burned my tongue intensely) then a quick bite of watermelon and I felt immediate relief. Oddly, drinking water, even though it was alkaline, burned my tongue as if I was swallowing fire. Do whatever it takes to keep your weight up. Until I found that watermelon would allow me to consume food, at least in small amounts, I was 84 pounds and needed IV nutrients administered by a Home Care Nurse. Yep, let's try to avoid that from happening if at all possible.

-Skincare

Use an antioxidant serum to fight against free radicals that occur within the skin due to UV light, radiation therapy, chemotherapy, and other factors, including diet. I recommend using zinc-based sun protection on any exposed areas. Select SPF 30 at least and reapply as needed (every 2 hours typically). Always be mindful of any allergies you may have when choosing products.

In addition, hyper-pigmentation can sometimes occur, especially when undergoing radiation therapy. The remedy is to use a safe, gentle exfoliant on the affected areas.

As a Holistic Esthetician and Energy Worker, I try to update my website from time to time as I change and grow to continue providing helpful information. I encourage you to check in at www.corehealingessentials.com to stay current with the most recent updates – including information about my laser-empowered, crystal-infused, organic Vibrational Enhancement Formulas. They are designed to help one process through undigested emotions and experience greater peace and mindbody balance.

Chapter 12
In Summation

I t's all about trust. Trusting Spiritual Guidance, trusting your "A-Team," and trusting that what is occurring is occurring for a reason. Since we're usually on a need-to-know basis, don't worry about the "why," just show up for yourself in all aspects, accept all the support that the Universe is going to supply and the outcome will be exactly what it's supposed to be.

Fulfilling our Soul's purpose is accomplished by living in the higher frequency realm. This state of elevated existence makes us feel better in all aspects of our being and allows us to be a beacon of light.

Emotions from the past and the present will arise during your journey. The fear, anger, sadness, confusion, etc. is inevitable; just go with it and see where it leads. I don't mean dwell in these emotions but do explore them; you just may find the key to your life story.

You are "Number One" while on this path…don't feel guilty about that; it's what's intended. This journey is an exploration into your Mindbody, and if you find the strength and determination to keep pushing through (to the best of your ability), you will find your truth. My belief is that we all manifest into human form from Spirit to learn lessons that will elevate us to the next level (if we need to) and to share our special gifts with the world, whatever they may be. Sometimes through crisis we learn what those gifts are and how best to offer them to the world.

Honor yourself and the process of life. Live as authentically as you can while accepting all the gifts that are available to you. Live from your heart as much as possible and be an observer of your ego and how it operates, then keep it in check. Decide to give life your all, but spend your energy wisely. Eat well, rest, exercise to the best of your ability to keep your blood flowing, meditate to receive Guidance and appreciate all that you have in your life—yes, even the illness. Gratitude is one of the most important emotions we can express; the more grateful we are, the more gifts we receive. There is a very sophisticated accounting system in this Universe, perhaps it's called Karma.

Give yourself a fighting chance by strengthening your Mindbody (either before you begin mainstream treatment or during) if you're choosing that path to wellness. It made the greatest sense to rid my Mindbody of accumulated waste and flood it with excellent nutrition to increase cellular energy. Consider the fact that cancer doesn't arise because we're deficient in chemotherapy drugs, so put into your body what it may be deficient in and watch how your cells start to respond.

It is important to find medical and non-medical practitioners that you trust who will guide you while you are on your very special journey. Accept support from whoever can truly support you with an open heart and a listening ear. Be open to suggestions, but make decisions based on your Spiritual Guidance and the knowledge of your medical professionals (I always had a sense that my A-Team was spiritually guided as well).

Thank you for allowing me to share my experience with you. My greatest hope is that you come to appreciate just how much God, The Universe, the Higher Self (whatever term or image resonates) loves you, supports you and wants you to fulfill your purpose. We have the tools we need at our fingertips, it's just a matter of living with the highest level of awareness and not allowing medical professionals, family, friends, or anyone else dictate our decisions. It's your life, your journey, so live it on your terms. Remember that all around you is a field of possibility.

I pray that *The Empowered Cancer Journey* inspires you and assists you on your very unique path to healing. Remember to keep Knowing, Doing, Surviving so that you may inspire others to do the same.

*I would consider myself privileged to know how this book may have inspired you, even in a subtle way, as you progress on your personal journey. If it feels right, contact me at carol@corehealingessentials.com and please be so kind as to specify whether I have your permission to share your blessed story (without providing your identity) in a blog posting or any other publication. We are all here to inspire each other, and never is it more important to do so as when the health of our Mindbody is at stake.

Namaste

Chapter 13
Gratitude – The Key to Abundance in Health, Wealth and Wisdom

Expressing gratitude for all of our Divine blessings is an empowering practice. I have provided this special section for you to do so, and I encourage you to continue this practice daily, if possible. Creating an "attractor field" full of positivity will yield a happier, more harmonious, and more abundant life.

I recommend starting with listing five things for which you are grateful, and before you know it, you won't be able to stop acknowledging all of your blessings.

Think about how your thoughts and writings will impact not only you, but the collective consciousness as well!

Begin here:

_____
_____
_____
_____
_____
_____

Creative Acknowledgements

I would like to acknowledge and express a very special thank you to Elizabeth Gervais, whose precise editing and formatting skills made all the difference in this project and to Alanna Tomer, whose creative genius produced an outstanding cover that reflects my light-filled experience.

-Space For Additional Notes-

51741945R00066

Made in the USA
Middletown, DE
04 July 2019